BUY THE TRUTH, AND SELL IT NOT; ALSO WISDOM, AND INSTRUCTION, AND UNDERSTANDING

BUY THE TRUTH, AND SELL IT NOT; ALSO WISDOM, AND INSTRUCTION, AND UNDERSTANDING

Compiled by Eugene Carvalho

To the Body of Christ.
May this compilation bless you richly!
With love…

TABLE OF CONTENTS

PURPOSE AND ACKNOWLEDGEMENTS

The Infallible, immutable, everlasting, eternal Word of God informs us that the Holy Spirit gives gifts to men and women of the Body of Christ. It states: "the gifts edify the body for the building up of the saints" (Eph. 4:12). I hope the talents and gifts the Lord has given me will be a blessing to someone else through the reading of this compilation.

I am grateful for the love I have received from family members, especially my wife Mercedes. I am also grateful for the knowledge, wisdom and love of many pastors, teachers, and saints that the Lord has used to bless me.

BUY THE TRUTH, AND SELL IT NOT; ALSO WISDOM, AND INSTRUCTION, AND UNDERSTANDING

Jesus said, "If ye continue in my word, then are ye my disciples indeed and ye shall know the truth, and the truth shall make you free" (Jn. 8:31-32 KJV). The truth brings revelation, revelation brings faith, and faith brings God on the scene. And faith is needed to please Him (Heb. 11:6).

The Bible says, "Neither shall they say, Lo here! or, lo there! for, behold, the kingdom of God is within you" (Lk. 17:21 KJV). With the kingdom of God and His Word in us, we should not lack Godly wisdom, instruction, or understanding. That's if we learn to live from the inside out. "Many people get all emotional. That's driven from the outside. Your emotions are supposed to follow you, not lead you. You cannot be driven by what is going on in the world. Satan has so much going on in the media and movies. He tries to drive people's thinking. And you become a threat to Satan because you have another channel by which you get your ideas."[1]

I went into a store to use a copy machine. The man started screaming at me loud regarding how to use it. I replied softly, thank you sir. Is there anything else you can tell me so I can be a better customer? You can disarm them with love.

---

[1] Quote by Dr. Bill Winston.

An important spiritual discipline in one's life should be a daily study of the Scriptures. The process of studying and meditating on the Word of God allows the mind to be renewed and Christians to become transformed into the image of Christ. The apostle Paul informs the brethren that individuals are transformed by the renewal of the mind (Ro. 12:2). He also tells them, "Finally, brethren, whatever is true, whatever is honorable, whatever is right, whatever is pure, whatever is lovely, whatever is of good repute, if there is any excellence and if anything worthy of praise, dwell on these things" (Php. 4:8).[2] A saint's mind needs to remain pure and holy through meditating on the Scriptures. There is no substitute on earth.

Every day I spend a great deal of time in my Bible to receive fresh revelation and insight which builds my faith, strengthens me and allows me to receive Godly wisdom. Without a daily study of God's Word an individual is setting themselves up for a life of self-destruction. The Scriptures are the only weapon at a Christian's disposal to combat the world, the flesh, and the devil and his entire host. Nothing else can transform and equip the soldiers of Christ for battle more than the discipline of study.

With that being said, let's investigate New Testament scriptures that discuss truth, wisdom, instruction, and understanding.

---

[2] All Scripture quotations, unless otherwise noted, are from the *New American Standard Bible.*

TRUTH IN THE NEW TESTAMENT

IN THE BOOK OF MATTHEW

Teach the Way of God in Truth

"Then the Pharisees went and plotted together how they might trap Him in what He said. And they sent their disciples to Him, along with the Herodians, saying, 'Teacher, we know that You are truthful and teach the way of God in truth, and defer to no one; for You are not partial to any. Tell us then, what do You think? Is it lawful to give a poll-tax to Caesar, or not?' But Jesus perceived their malice, and said, 'Why are you testing Me, you hypocrites? Show Me the coin used for the poll-tax.' And they brought Him a denarius. And He said to them, 'Whose likeness and inscription is this?' They said to Him, 'Caesar's' Then He *said to them, 'Then render to Caesar the things that are Caesar's; and to God the things that are God's.' And hearing this, they were amazed, and leaving Him, they went away" (Mt. 22:15-22).

IN THE BOOK OF MARK

Told Him the Whole Truth

"A woman who had had a hemorrhage for twelve years, and had endured much at the hands of many physicians, and had spent all that she had and was not helped at all, but rather had grown worse — after hearing about Jesus, she came up in the crowd behind Him and touched His cloak. For she thought, 'If I just touch His garments, I will get well.' Immediately the flow of her blood was dried up; and she felt in her body that she was healed of her affliction. Immediately Jesus, perceiving in Himself that the power proceeding from Him had gone forth, turned around in the crowd and said, 'Who touched My garments?' And His disciples said to Him, 'You see the crowd pressing in on You, and You say, "Who touched Me?"' And He looked around to see the woman who had done this. But the woman fearing and trembling, aware of what had happened to her, came and fell down before Him and told Him the whole truth. And He said to her, "Daughter, your faith has made you well; go in peace and be healed of your affliction'" (Mr. 5:25-34).

Teach the Way of God in Truth

"Then they sent some of the Pharisees and Herodians to Him in order to trap Him in a statement. They came and said to Him, 'Teacher, we know that You are truthful and defer to no one; for You are not partial to any, but teach the way of God in truth. Is it lawful to pay a poll-tax to Caesar, or not? Shall we pay or shall we not pay?' But He, knowing their hypocrisy, said to them, 'Why are you testing Me? Bring Me a denarius to look at.' They brought one. And He said to them, 'Whose likeness and inscription is this?' And they said to Him, "Caesar's.' And Jesus said to them, 'Render to Caesar the things that are Caesar's, and to God the things that are God's.' And they were amazed at Him" (Mr. 12:13-17).

IN THE BOOK OF LUKE

The Exact Truth About Things

"Inasmuch as many have undertaken to compile an account of the things accomplished among us, just as they were handed down to us by those who from the beginning were eyewitnesses and servants of the word, it seemed fitting for me as well, having investigated everything carefully from the beginning, to write it out for you in consecutive order, most excellent Theophilus; so that you may know the exact truth about the things you have been taught" (Lk.. 1:1-4).

I Say to You in Truth

"And He said, 'Truly I say to you, no prophet is welcome in his hometown. But I say to you in truth, there were many widows in Israel in the days of Elijah, when the sky was shut up for three years and six months, when a great famine came over all the land; and yet Elijah was sent to none of them, but only to Zarephath, in the land of Sidon, to a woman who was a widow. And there were many lepers in Israel in the time of Elisha the prophet; and none of them was cleansed, but only Naaman the Syrian.' And all the people in the synagogue were filled with rage as they heard these things; and they got up and drove Him out of the city, and led Him to the brow of the hill on which their city had been built, in order to throw Him down the cliff. But passing through their midst, He went His way" (Lu. 4:24-30).

In Truth

"The scribes and the chief priests tried to lay hands on Him that very hour, and they feared the people; for they understood that He spoke this parable against them. So they watched Him, and sent spies who pretended to be righteous, in order that they might catch Him in some statement, so that they could deliver Him to the rule and the authority of the governor. They questioned Him, saying, 'Teacher, we know that You speak and teach correctly, and You are not partial to any, but teach the way of God in truth. Is it lawful for us to pay taxes to Caesar, or not? But He detected their trickery and said to them, 'Show Me a denarius. Whose likeness and inscription does it have?' They said, 'Caesar's.' And He said to them, 'Then render to Caesar the things that are Caesar's, and to God the things that are God's.' And they were unable to catch Him in a saying in the presence of the people; and being amazed at His answer, they became silent" (Lu. 20:19-26).

Chapter Two

IN THE BOOK OF JOHN

Full of Grace and Truth

"And the Word became flesh, and dwelt among us, and we saw His glory, glory as of the only begotten from the Father, full of grace and truth. John testified about Him and cried out, saying, 'This was He of whom I said, "He who comes after me has a higher rank than I, for He existed before me.'" For of His fullness we have all received, and grace upon grace. For the Law was given through Moses; grace and truth were realized through Jesus Christ" (Jn. 1:14-17).

He Who Practices the Truth Comes to the Light

"For God so loved the world, that He gave His only begotten Son, that whoever believes in Him shall not perish, but have eternal life. For God did not send the Son into the world to judge the world, but that the world might be saved through Him. He who believes in Him is not judged; he who does not believe has been judged already, because he has not believed in the name of the only begotten Son of God. This is the judgment, that the Light has come into the world, and men loved the darkness rather than the Light, for their deeds were evil. For everyone who does evil hates the Light, and does not come to the Light for fear that his deeds will be exposed. But he who practices the truth comes to the Light, so that his deeds may be manifested as having been wrought in God" (Jn. 3:16-21).

Will Worship the Father in Spirit and Truth

"The woman said to Him, 'Sir, give me this water, so I will not be thirsty nor come all the way here to draw.' He said to her, 'Go, call your husband and come here." The woman answered and said, 'I have no husband.' Jesus said to her, 'You have correctly said, "I have no husband"; for you have had five husbands, and the one whom you now have is not your husband; this you have said truly." The woman said to Him, 'Sir, I perceive that You are a prophet. Our fathers worshiped in this mountain, and you people say that in Jerusalem is the place where men ought to worship.' Jesus said to her, 'Woman, believe Me, an hour is coming when neither in this mountain nor in Jerusalem will you worship the Father. You worship what you do not know; we worship what we know, for salvation is from the Jews. But an hour is coming, and now is, when the true worshipers will worship the Father in spirit and truth; for such people the Father seeks to be His worshipers. God is spirit, and those who worship Him must worship in spirit and truth.' The woman said to Him, 'I know that Messiah is coming (He who is called Christ); when that One comes, He will declare all things to us.' Jesus said to her, 'I who speak to you am He'" (Jn. 4:15-26).

Chapter Two

He Has Testified to the Truth

"If I alone testify about Myself, My testimony is not true. There is another who testifies of Me, and I know that the testimony which He gives about Me is true. You have sent to John, and he has testified to the truth. But the testimony which I receive is not from man, but I say these things so that you may be saved. He was the lamp that was burning and was shining and you were willing to rejoice for a while in his light. But the testimony which I have is greater than the testimony of John; for the works which the Father has given Me to accomplish — the very works that I do — testify about Me, that the Father has sent Me. And the Father who sent Me, He has testified of Me. You have neither heard His voice at any time nor seen His form. You do not have His word abiding in you, for you do not believe Him whom He sent. You search the Scriptures because you think that in them you have eternal life; it is these that testify about Me; and you are unwilling to come to Me so that you may have life. I do not receive glory from men; but I know you, that you do not have the love of God in yourselves. I have come in My Father's name, and you do not receive Me; if another comes in his own name, you will receive him. How can you believe, when you receive glory from one another and you do not seek the glory that is from the one and only God? Do not think that I will accuse you before the Father; the one who accuses you is Moses, in whom you have set your hope. For if you believed Moses, you would believe Me, for he wrote about Me. But if you do not believe his writings, how will you believe My words" (Jn. 5:31-47)?

The Truth Will Make You Free

"So Jesus was saying to those Jews who had believed Him, 'If you continue in My word, then you are truly disciples of Mine; and you will know the truth, and the truth will make you free.' They answered Him, 'We are Abraham's descendants and have never yet been enslaved to anyone; how is it that You say, "You will become free'"" (Jn. 8:31-33)?

A Man Who Has Told You the Truth

"They answered and said to Him, 'Abraham is our father.' Jesus said to them, 'If you are Abraham's children, do the deeds of Abraham. But as it is, you are seeking to kill Me, a man who has told you the truth, which I heard from God; this Abraham did not do. You are doing the deeds of your father.' They said to Him, 'We were not born of fornication; we have one Father: God.' Jesus said to them, 'If God were your Father, you would love Me, for I proceeded forth and have come from God, for I have not even come on My own initiative, but He sent Me. Why do you not understand what I am saying? It is because you cannot hear My word. You are of your father the devil, and you want to do the desires of your father. He was a murderer from the beginning, and does not stand in the truth because there is no truth in him. Whenever he speaks a lie, he speaks from his own nature, for he is a liar and the father of lies. But because I speak the truth, you do not believe Me. Which one of you convicts Me of sin? If I speak truth, why do you not believe Me? He who is of God hears the words of God; for this reason you do not hear them, because you are not of God'" (Jn. 8:39-47).

I Am the Way, and the Truth, and the Life

"Do not let your heart be troubled; believe in God, believe also in Me. In My Father's house are many dwelling places; if it were not so, I would have told you; for I go to prepare a place for you. If I go and prepare a place for you, I will come again and receive you to Myself, that where I am, there you may be also. And you know the way where I am going. Thomas said to Him, 'Lord, we do not know where You are going, how do we know the way?' Jesus said to him, 'I am the way, and the truth, and the life; no one comes to the Father but through Me. If you had known Me, you would have known My Father also; from now on you know Him, and have seen Him'" (Jn. 14:1-7).

Chapter Two

The Spirit of Truth

"If you love Me, you will keep My commandments. I will ask the Father, and He will give you another Helper, that He may be with you forever; that is the Spirit of truth, whom the world cannot receive, because it does not see Him or know Him, but you know Him because He abides with you and will be in you" (Jn. 14:15-17).

The Helper, the Spirit of Truth Who Proceeds from the Father

"When the Helper comes, whom I will send to you from the Father, that is the Spirit of truth who proceeds from the Father, He will testify about Me, and you will testify also, because you have been with Me from the beginning" (Jn. 15:26-27).

I Tell You the Truth, It Is to Your Advantage

"But now I am going to Him who sent Me; and none of you asks Me, "Where are You going?" But because I have said these things to you, sorrow has filled your heart. But I tell you the truth, it is to your advantage that I go away; for if I do not go away, the Helper will not come to you; but if I go, I will send Him to you. And He, when He comes, will convict the world concerning sin and righteousness and judgment; concerning sin, because they do not believe in Me; and concerning righteousness, because I go to the Father and you no longer see Me; and concerning judgment, because the ruler of this world has been judged" (Jn. 16:5-11).

But When He, the Spirit of Truth, Comes

"I have many more things to say to you, but you cannot bear them now. But when He, the Spirit of truth, comes, He will guide you into all the truth; for He will not speak on His own initiative, but whatever He hears, He will speak; and He will disclose to you what is to come. He will glorify Me, for He will take of Mine and will disclose it to you. All things that the Father has are Mine; therefore I said that He takes of Mine and will disclose it to you" (Jn. 16:12-15).

Sanctify Them in the Truth

"But now I come to You; and these things I speak in the world so that they may have My joy made full in themselves. I have given them Your word; and the world has hated them, because they are not of the world, even as I am not of the world. I do not ask You to take them out of the world, but to keep them from the evil one. They are not of the world, even as I am not of the world. Sanctify them in the truth; Your word is truth. As You sent Me into the world, I also have sent them into the world. For their sakes I sanctify Myself, that they themselves also may be sanctified in truth" (Jn.

17:13-19).

Everyone Who Is of the Truth Hears My Voice

"Therefore Pilate entered again into the Praetorium, and summoned Jesus and said to Him, 'Are You the King of the Jews?' Jesus answered, 'Are you saying this on your own initiative, or did others tell you about Me?' Pilate answered, 'I am not a Jew, am I? Your own nation and the chief priests delivered You to me; what have You done?' Jesus answered, 'My kingdom is not of this world. If My kingdom were of this world, then My servants would be fighting so that I would not be handed over to the Jews; but as it is, My kingdom is not of this realm.' Therefore Pilate said to Him, 'So You are a king?' Jesus answered, 'You say correctly that I am a king. For this I have been born, and for this I have come into the world, to testify to the truth. Everyone who is of the truth hears My voice.' Pilate said to Him, 'What is truth?' And when he had said this, he went out again to the Jews and said to them, 'I find no guilt in Him'" (Jn. 18:33-38).

He Is Telling the Truth

"Then the Jews, because it was the day of preparation, so that the bodies would not remain on the cross on the Sabbath (for that Sabbath was a high day), asked Pilate that their legs might be broken, and that they might be taken away. So the soldiers came, and broke the legs of the first man and of the other who was crucified with Him; but coming to Jesus, when they saw that He was already dead, they did not break His legs. But one of the soldiers pierced His side with a spear, and immediately blood and water came out. And he who has seen has testified, and his testimony is true; and he knows that he is telling the truth, so that you also may believe. For these things came to pass to fulfill the Scripture, 'NOT A BONE OF HIM SHALL BE BROKEN.' And again another Scripture says, 'THEY SHALL LOOK ON HIM WHOM THEY PIERCED'" (Jn. 19:31-37).

IN THE BOOK OF ACTS

I Utter Words of Sober Truth

"While Paul was saying this in his defense, Festus *said in a loud voice, 'Paul, you are out of your mind! Your great learning is driving you mad.' But Paul said, 'I am not out of my mind, most excellent Festus, but I utter words of sober truth. For the king knows about these matters, and I speak to him also with confidence, since I am persuaded that none of these things escape his notice; for this has not been done in a corner. King Agrippa, do you believe the Prophets? I know that you do.' Agrippa replied to Paul, 'In a short time you will persuade me to become a Christian.' And Paul said, 'I would wish to God, that whether in a short or long time, not only you, but also all who hear me this day, might become such as I am, except for these chains'" (Ac. 26:24-29).

IN THE BOOK OF ROMANS

Men Who Suppress the Truth in Unrighteousness

"For the wrath of God is revealed from heaven against all ungodliness and unrighteousness of men who suppress the truth in unrighteousness, because that which is known about God is evident within them; for God made it evident to them. For since the creation of the world His invisible attributes, His eternal power and divine nature, have been clearly seen, being understood through what has been made, so that they are without excuse. For even though they knew God, they did not honor Him as God or give thanks, but they became futile in their speculations, and their foolish heart was darkened. Professing to be wise, they became fools, and exchanged the glory of the incorruptible God for an image in the form of corruptible man and of birds and four-footed animals and crawling creatures" (Ro 1:18-23).

They Exchanged the Truth of God for a Lie

"Therefore God gave them over in the lusts of their hearts to impurity, so that their bodies would be dishonored among them. For they exchanged the truth of God for a lie, and worshiped and served the creature rather than the Creator, who is blessed forever. Amen" (Ro. 1:24-25).

Selfishly Ambitious and Do Not Obey the Truth

"Therefore you have no excuse, everyone of you who passes judgment, for in that which you judge another, you condemn yourself; for you who judge practice the same things. And we know that the judgment of God rightly falls upon those who practice such things. But do you suppose this, O man, when you pass judgment on those who practice such things and do the same yourself, that you will escape the judgment of God? Or do you think lightly of the riches of His kindness and tolerance and patience, not knowing that the kindness of God leads you to repentance? But because of your stubbornness and unrepentant heart you are storing up wrath for yourself in the day of wrath and revelation of the righteous judgment of God, who WILL RENDER TO EACH PERSON ACCORDING TO HIS DEEDS: to those who by perseverance in doing good seek for glory and honor and immortality, eternal life; but to those who are selfishly ambitious and do not obey the truth, but obey unrighteousness, wrath and indignation. There will be tribulation and distress for every soul of man who does evil, of the Jew first and also of the Greek, but glory and honor and peace to everyone who does good, to the Jew first and also to the Greek. For there is no partiality with God" (Ro. 2:1-11).

The Embodiment of Knowledge and of the Truth

"But if you bear the name 'Jew' and rely upon the Law and boast in God, and know His will and approve the things that are essential, being instructed out of the Law, and are confident that you yourself are a guide to the blind, a light to those who are in darkness, a corrector of the foolish, a teacher of the immature, having in the Law the embodiment of knowledge and of the truth, you, therefore, who teach another, do you not teach yourself? You who preach that one shall not steal, do you steal? You who say that one should not commit adultery, do you commit adultery? You who abhor idols, do you rob temples? You who boast in the Law, through your breaking the Law, do you dishonor God? For 'THE NAME OF GOD IS BLASPHEMED AMONG THE GENTILES BECAUSE OF YOU,' just as it is written" (Ro. 2:17-24).

He Truth of God Abounded to His Glory

"Then what advantage has the Jew? Or what is the benefit of circumcision? Great in every respect. First of all, that they were entrusted with the oracles of God. What then? If some did not believe, their unbelief will not nullify the faithfulness of God, will it? May it never be!

Rather, let God be found true, though every man be found a liar, as it is written, 'THAT YOU MAY BE JUSTIFIED IN YOUR WORDS, AND PREVAIL WHEN YOU ARE JUDGED.' But if our unrighteousness demonstrates the righteousness of God, what shall we say? The God who inflicts wrath is not unrighteous, is He? (I am speaking in human terms.) May it never be! For otherwise, how will God judge the world? But if through my lie the truth of God abounded to His glory, why am I also still being judged as a sinner? And why not say (as we are slanderously reported and as some claim that we say), 'Let us do evil that good may come'? Their condemnation is just" (Ro. 3:1-8).

I Am Telling the Truth in Christ

"I am telling the truth in Christ, I am not lying, my conscience testifies with me in the Holy Spirit, that I have great sorrow and unceasing grief in my heart. For I could wish that I myself were accursed, separated from Christ for the sake of my brethren, my kinsmen according to the flesh, who are Israelites, to whom belongs the adoption as sons, and the glory and the covenants and the giving of the Law and the temple service and the promises, whose are the fathers, and from whom is the Christ according to the flesh, who is over all, God blessed forever. Amen" (Ro. 9:1-5).

On Behalf of the Truth of God

"Therefore, accept one another, just as Christ also accepted us to the glory of God. For I say that Christ has become a servant to the circumcision on behalf of the truth of God to confirm the promises given to the fathers, and for the Gentiles to glorify God for His mercy; as it is written, 'THEREFORE I WILL GIVE PRAISE TO YOU AMONG THE GENTILES, AND I WILL SING TO YOUR NAME.' Again he says, 'REJOICE, O GENTILES, WITH HIS PEOPLE.' And again, 'PRAISE THE LORD ALL YOU GENTILES, AND LET ALL THE PEOPLES PRAISE HIM.' Again Isaiah says, 'THERE SHALL COME THE ROOT OF JESSE, AND HE WHO ARISES TO RULE OVER THE GENTILES, IN HIM SHALL THE GENTILES HOPE.' Now may the God of hope fill you with all joy and peace in believing, so that you will abound in hope by the power of the Holy Spirit" (Ro. 15:7-13).

IN THE BOOK OF 1 CORINTHIANS

With the Unleavened Bread of Sincerity and Truth

"Your boasting is not good. Do you not know that a little leaven leavens the whole lump of dough? Clean out the old leaven so that you may be a new lump, just as you are in fact unleavened. For Christ our Passover also has been sacrificed. Therefore let us celebrate the feast, not with old leaven, nor with the leaven of malice and wickedness, but with the unleavened bread of sincerity and truth" (1Co. 5:6-8).

Rejoices with the Truth

"Love is patient, love is kind and is not jealous; love does not brag and is not arrogant, does not act unbecomingly; it does not seek its own, is not provoked, does not take into account a wrong suffered, does not rejoice in unrighteousness, but rejoices with the truth; bears all things, believes all things, hopes all things, endures all things" (1Co. 13:4-7).

IN THE BOOK OF 2 CORINTHIANS

By the Manifestation of Truth

"Therefore, since we have this ministry, as we received mercy, we do not lose heart, but we have renounced the things hidden because of shame, not walking in craftiness or adulterating the word of God, but by the manifestation of truth commending ourselves to every man's conscience in the sight of God. And even if our gospel is veiled, it is veiled to those who are perishing, in whose case the god of this world has blinded the minds of the unbelieving so that they might not see the light of the gospel of the glory of Christ, who is the image of God. For we do not preach ourselves but Christ Jesus as Lord, and ourselves as your bond-servants for Jesus' sake. For God, who said, 'Light shall shine out of darkness,' is the One who has shone in our hearts to give the Light of the knowledge of the glory of God in the face of Christ" (2Co.4:1-6).

In the Word of Truth

"And working together with Him, we also urge you not to receive the grace of God in vain — for He says, 'AT THE ACCEPTABLE TIME I LISTENED TO YOU, AND ON THE DAY OF SALVATION I HELPED YOU.' Behold, now is 'THE ACCEPTABLE TIME,' behold, now is 'THE DAY OF SALVATION' — giving no cause for offense in anything, so that the ministry will not be discredited, but in everything commending ourselves as servants of God, in much endurance, in afflictions, in hardships, in distresses, in beatings, in imprisonments, in tumults, in labors, in sleeplessness, in hunger, in purity, in knowledge, in patience, in kindness, in the Holy Spirit, in genuine love, in the word of truth, in the power of God; by the weapons of righteousness for the right hand and the left, by glory and dishonor, by evil report and good report; regarded as deceivers and yet true; as unknown yet well-known, as dying yet behold, we live; as punished yet not put to death, as sorrowful yet always rejoicing, as poor yet making many rich, as having nothing yet possessing all things" (2Co. 6:1-10).

We Spoke All Things to You in Truth

"For even when we came into Macedonia our flesh had no rest, but we were afflicted on every side: conflicts without, fears within. But God, who comforts the depressed, comforted us by the coming of Titus; and not only by his coming, but also by the comfort with which he was comforted in you, as he reported to us your longing, your mourning, your zeal for me; so that I rejoiced even more. For though I caused you sorrow by my letter, I do not regret it; though I did regret it — for I see that that letter caused you sorrow, though only for a while —I now rejoice, not that you were made sorrowful, but that you were made sorrowful to the point of repentance; for you were made sorrowful according to the will of God, so that you might not suffer loss in anything through us. For the sorrow that is according to the will of God produces a repentance without regret, leading to salvation, but the sorrow of the world produces death. For behold what earnestness this very thing, this godly sorrow, has produced in you: what vindication of yourselves, what indignation, what fear, what longing, what zeal, what avenging of wrong! In everything you demonstrated yourselves to be innocent in the matter. So although I wrote to you, it was not for the sake of the offender nor for the sake of the one offended, but that your earnestness on our behalf might be made known to you in the sight of God. For this reason we have been comforted. And besides our comfort, we rejoiced even much more for the joy of Titus, because his spirit has been refreshed by you all. For if in anything I have boasted to him about you, I was not put to shame; but as we spoke all things to you in truth, so also our boasting before Titus proved to be the truth. His affection abounds all the more toward you, as he remembers the obedience of you all, how you received him with fear and trembling. I rejoice that in everything I have confidence in you" (2Co. 7:5-16).

The Truth of Christ Is in Me

"Or did I commit a sin in humbling myself so that you might be exalted, because I preached the gospel of God to you without charge? I robbed other churches by taking wages from them to serve you; and when I was present with you and was in need, I was not a burden to anyone; for when the brethren came from Macedonia they fully supplied my need, and in everything I kept myself from being a burden to you, and will continue to do so. As the truth of Christ is in me, this boasting of mine will not be stopped in the regions of Achaia. Why? Because I do not love you? God knows I do" (2Co. 11:7-11)!

I Will Be Speaking the Truth

"Boasting is necessary, though it is not profitable; but I will go on to visions and revelations of the Lord. I know a man in Christ who fourteen years ago — whether in the body I do not know, or out of the body I do not know, God knows — such a man was caught up to the third heaven. And I know how such a man — whether in the body or apart from the body I do not know, God knows —was caught up into Paradise and heard inexpressible words, which a man is not permitted to speak. On behalf of such a man I will boast; but on my own behalf I will not boast, except in regard to my weaknesses. For if I do wish to boast I will not be foolish, for I will be speaking the truth; but I refrain from this, so that no one will credit me with more than he sees in me or hears from me. Because of the surpassing greatness of the revelations, for this reason, to keep me from exalting myself, there was given me a thorn in the flesh, a messenger of Satan to torment me — to keep me from exalting myself! Concerning this I implored the Lord three times that it might leave me. And He has said to me, 'My grace is sufficient for you, for power is perfected in weakness.' Most gladly, therefore, I will rather boast about my weaknesses, so that the power of Christ may dwell in me. Therefore I am well content with weaknesses, with insults, with distresses, with persecutions, with difficulties, for Christ's sake; for when I am weak, then I am strong" (2Co. 12:1-10).

We Can Do Nothing Against the Truth

"Test yourselves to see if you are in the faith; examine yourselves! Or do you not recognize this about yourselves, that Jesus Christ is in you — unless indeed you fail the test? But I trust that you will realize that we ourselves do not fail the test. Now we pray to God that you do no wrong; not that we ourselves may appear approved, but that you may do what is right, even though we may appear unapproved. For we can do nothing against the truth, but only for the truth. For we rejoice when we ourselves are weak but you are strong; this we also pray for, that you be made complete. For this reason I am writing these things while absent, so that when present I need not use severity, in accordance with the authority which the Lord gave me for building up and not for tearing down" (2Co. 13:5-10).

IN THE BOOK OF GALATIANS

So That the Truth of the Gospel Would Remain

"Then after an interval of fourteen years I went up again to Jerusalem with Barnabas, taking Titus along also. It was because of a revelation that I went up; and I submitted to them the gospel which I preach among the Gentiles, but I did so in private to those who were of reputation, for fear that I might be running, or had run, in vain. But not even Titus, who was with me, though he was a Greek, was compelled to be circumcised. But it was because of the false brethren secretly brought in, who had sneaked in to spy out our liberty which we have in Christ Jesus, in order to bring us into bondage. But we did not yield in subjection to them for even an hour, so that the truth of the gospel would remain with you. But from those who were of high reputation (what they were makes no difference to me; God shows no partiality) — well, those who were of reputation contributed nothing to me. But on the contrary, seeing that I had been entrusted with the gospel to the uncircumcised, just as Peter had been to the circumcised (for He who effectually worked for Peter in his apostleship to the circumcised effectually worked for me also to the Gentiles), and recognizing the grace that had been given to me, James and Cephas and John, who were reputed to be pillars, gave to me and Barnabas the right hand of fellowship, so that we might go to the Gentiles and they to the circumcised. They only asked us to remember the poor — the very thing I also was eager to do" (Gal. 2:1-10).

Straightforward About the Truth of the Gospel

"But when Cephas came to Antioch, I opposed him to his face, because he stood condemned. For prior to the coming of certain men from James, he used to eat with the Gentiles;

but when they came, he began to withdraw and hold himself aloof, fearing the party of the circumcision. The rest of the Jews joined him in hypocrisy, with the result that even Barnabas was carried away by their hypocrisy. But when I saw that they were not straightforward about the truth of the gospel, I said to Cephas in the presence of all, 'If you, being a Jew, live like the Gentiles and not like the Jews, how is it that you compel the Gentiles to live like Jews'" (Gal. 2:11-14)?

I Become Your Enemy by Telling You the Truth?

"I beg of you, brethren, become as I am, for I also have become as you are. You have done me no wrong; but you know that it was because of a bodily illness that I preached the gospel to you the first time; and that which was a trial to you in my bodily condition you did not despise or loathe, but you received me as an angel of God, as Christ Jesus Himself. Where then is that sense of blessing you had? For I bear you witness that, if possible, you would have plucked out your eyes and given them to me. So have I become your enemy by telling you the truth? They eagerly seek you, not commendably, but they wish to shut you out so that you will seek them. But it is good always to be eagerly sought in a commendable manner, and not only when I am present with you. My children, with whom I am again in labor until Christ is formed in you — but I could wish to be present with you now and to change my tone, for I am perplexed about you" (Gal. 4:12-20).

Who Hindered You from Obeying the Truth?

"You were running well; who hindered you from obeying the truth? This persuasion did not come from Him who calls you. A little leaven leavens the whole lump of dough. I have confidence in you in the Lord that you will adopt no other view; but the one who is disturbing you will bear his judgment, whoever he is. But I, brethren, if I still preach circumcision, why am I still persecuted? Then the stumbling block of the cross has been abolished. I wish that those who are troubling you would even mutilate themselves" (Gal. 5:7-12).

IN THE BOOK OF EPHESIANS

After Listening to the Message of Truth

"Blessed be the God and Father of our Lord Jesus Christ, who has blessed us with every spiritual blessing in the heavenly places in Christ, just as He chose us in Him before the foundation of the world, that we would be holy and blameless before Him. In love He predestined us to adoption as sons through Jesus Christ to Himself, according to the kind intention of His will, to the praise of the glory of His grace, which He freely bestowed on us in the Beloved. In Him we have redemption through His blood, the forgiveness of our trespasses, according to the riches of His grace which He lavished on us. In all wisdom and insight He made known to us the mystery of His will, according to His kind intention which He purposed in Him with a view to an administration suitable to the fullness of the times, that is, the summing up of all things in Christ, things in the heavens and things on the earth. In Him also we have obtained an inheritance, having been predestined according to His purpose who works all things after the counsel of His will, to the end that we who were the first to hope in Christ would be to the praise of His glory. In Him, you also, after listening to the message of truth, the gospel of your salvation — having also believed, you were sealed in Him with the Holy Spirit of promise, who is given as a pledge of our inheritance, with a view to the redemption of God's own possession, to the praise of His glory" (Eph. 1:3-14).

Speaking the Truth in Love

"Therefore I, the prisoner of the Lord, implore you to walk in a manner worthy of the calling with which you have been called, with all humility and gentleness, with patience, showing tolerance for one another in love, being diligent to preserve the unity of the Spirit in the bond of peace. There is one body and one Spirit, just as also you were called in one hope of your calling; one Lord, one faith, one baptism, one God and

Father of all who is over all and through all and in all. But to each one of us grace was given according to the measure of Christ's gift. Therefore it says, 'WHEN HE ASCENDED ON HIGH, HE LED CAPTIVE A HOST OF CAPTIVES, AND HE GAVE GIFTS TO MEN.' (Now this expression, 'He ascended,' what does it mean except that He also had descended into the lower parts of the earth? He who descended is Himself also He who ascended far above all the heavens, so that He might fill all things.) And He gave some as apostles, and some as prophets, and some as evangelists, and some as pastors and teachers, for the equipping of the saints for the work of service, to the building up of the body of Christ; until we all attain to the unity of the faith, and of the knowledge of the Son of God, to a mature man, to the measure of the stature which belongs to the fullness of Christ. As a result, we are no longer to be children, tossed here and there by waves and carried about by every wind of doctrine, by the trickery of men, by craftiness in deceitful scheming; but speaking the truth in love, we are to grow up in all aspects into Him who is the head, even Christ, from whom the whole body, being fitted and held together by what every joint supplies, according to the proper working of each individual part, causes the growth of the body for the building up of itself in love" (Eph. 4:1-16).

Chapter Two

Just as Truth Is in Jesus

"So this I say, and affirm together with the Lord, that you walk no longer just as the Gentiles also walk, in the futility of their mind, being darkened in their understanding, excluded from the life of God because of the ignorance that is in them, because of the hardness of their heart; and they, having become callous, have given themselves over to sensuality for the practice of every kind of impurity with greediness. But you did not learn Christ in this way, if indeed you have heard Him and have been taught in Him, just as truth is in Jesus, that, in reference to your former manner of life, you lay aside the old self, which is being corrupted in accordance with the lusts of deceit, and that you be renewed in the spirit of your mind, and put on the new self, which in the likeness of God has been created in righteousness and holiness of the truth" (Eph. 4:17-24).

Speak Truth Each One of You

"Therefore, laying aside falsehood, SPEAK TRUTH EACH ONE of you WITH HIS NEIGHBOR, for we are members of one another. BE ANGRY, AND yet DO NOT SIN; do not let the sun go down on your anger, and do not give the devil an opportunity. He who steals must steal no longer; but rather he must labor, performing with his own hands what is good, so that he will have something to share with one who has need. Let no unwholesome word proceed from your mouth, but only such a word as is good for edification according to the need of the moment, so that it will give grace to those who hear. Do not grieve the Holy Spirit of God, by whom you were sealed for the day of redemption. Let all bitterness and wrath and anger and clamor and slander be put away from you, along with all malice. Be kind to one another, tender-hearted, forgiving each other, just as God in Christ also has forgiven you" (Eph. 4:25-32).

Consists in all Goodness and Righteousness and Truth

"Let no one deceive you with empty words, for because of these things the wrath of God comes upon the sons of disobedience. Therefore do not be partakers with them; for you were formerly darkness, but now you are Light in the Lord; walk as children of Light (for the fruit of the Light consists in all goodness and righteousness and truth), trying to learn what is pleasing to the Lord. Do not participate in the unfruitful deeds of darkness, but instead even expose them; for it is disgraceful even to speak of the things which are done by them in secret. But all things become visible when they are exposed by the light, for everything that becomes visible is light. For this reason it says, 'Awake, sleeper, And arise from the dead, And Christ will shine on you'" (Eph. 5:6-14).

Having Girded Your Loins with Truth

"Finally, be strong in the Lord and in the strength of His might. Put on the full armor of God, so that you will be able to stand firm against the schemes of the devil. For our struggle is not against flesh and blood, but against the rulers, against the powers, against the world forces of this darkness, against the spiritual forces of wickedness in the heavenly places. Therefore, take up the full armor of God, so that you will be able to resist in the evil day, and having done everything, to stand firm. Stand firm therefore, HAVING GIRDED YOUR LOINS WITH TRUTH, and HAVING PUT ON THE BREASTPLATE OF RIGHTEOUSNESS, and having shod YOUR FEET WITH THE PREPARATION OF THE GOSPEL OF PEACE; in addition to all, taking up the shield of faith with which you will be able to extinguish all the flaming arrows of the evil one. And take THE HELMET OF SALVATION, and the sword of the Spirit, which is the word of God" (Eph. 6:10-17).

IN THE BOOK OF PHILIPPIANS

In Pretense or in Truth

"Now I want you to know, brethren, that my circumstances have turned out for the greater progress of the gospel, so that my imprisonment in the cause of Christ has become well known throughout the whole praetorian guard and to everyone else, and that most of the brethren, trusting in the Lord because of my imprisonment, have far more courage to speak the word of God without fear. Some, to be sure, are preaching Christ even from envy and strife, but some also from good will; the latter do it out of love, knowing that I am appointed for the defense of the gospel; the former proclaim Christ out of selfish ambition rather than from pure motives, thinking to cause me distress in my imprisonment. What then? Only that in every way, whether in pretense or in truth, Christ is proclaimed; and in this I rejoice. Yes, and I will rejoice, for I know that this will turn out for my deliverance through your prayers and the provision of the Spirit of Jesus Christ, according to my earnest expectation and hope, that I will not be put to shame in anything, but that with all boldness, Christ will even now, as always, be exalted in my body, whether by life or by death" (Php. 1:12-20).

IN THE BOOK OF COLOSSIANS

You Previously Heard in the Word of Truth

"We give thanks to God, the Father of our Lord Jesus Christ, praying always for you, since we heard of your faith in Christ Jesus and the love which you have for all the saints; because of the hope laid up for you in heaven, of which you previously heard in the word of truth, the gospel which has come to you, just as in all the world also it is constantly bearing fruit and increasing, even as it has been doing in you also since the day you heard of it and understood the grace of God in truth; just as you learned it from Epaphras, our beloved fellow bond-servant, who is a faithful servant of Christ on our behalf, and he also informed us of your love in the Spirit" (Col. 1:3-8).

IN THE BOOK OF 2 THESSALONIANS

They Did Not Receive the Love of the Truth

"Now we request you, brethren, with regard to the coming of our Lord Jesus Christ and our gathering together to Him, that you not be quickly shaken from your composure or be disturbed either by a spirit or a message or a letter as if from us, to the effect that the day of the Lord has come. Let no one in any way deceive you, for it will not come unless the apostasy comes first, and the man of lawlessness is revealed, the son of destruction, who opposes and exalts himself above every so-called god or object of worship, so that he takes his seat in the temple of God, displaying himself as being God. Do you not remember that while I was still with you, I was telling you these things? And you know what restrains him now, so that in his time he will be revealed. For the mystery of lawlessness is already at work; only he who now restrains will do so until he is taken out of the way. Then that lawless one will be revealed whom the Lord will slay with the breath of His mouth and bring to an end by the appearance of His coming; that is, the one whose coming is in accord with the activity of Satan, with all power and signs and false wonders, and with all the deception of wickedness for those who perish, because they did not receive the love of the truth so as to be saved. For this reason God will send upon them a deluding influence so that they will believe what is false, in order that they all may be judged who did not believe the truth, but took pleasure in wickedness" (2Th. 2:1-12).

Sanctification by the Spirit and Faith in the Truth

"But we should always give thanks to God for you, brethren beloved by the Lord, because God has chosen you from the beginning for salvation through sanctification by the Spirit and faith in the truth. It was for this He called you through our gospel, that you may gain the glory of our Lord Jesus Christ. So then, brethren, stand firm and hold to the traditions which you were taught, whether by word of mouth or by letter from us" (2Th. 2:13-15).

Chapter Two

IN THE BOOK OF 1 TIMOTHY

To Come to the Knowledge of the Truth

"First of all, then, I urge that entreaties and prayers, petitions and thanksgivings, be made on behalf of all men, for kings and all who are in authority, so that we may lead a tranquil and quiet life in all godliness and dignity. This is good and acceptable in the sight of God our Savior, who desires all men to be saved and to come to the knowledge of the truth. For there is one God, and one mediator also between God and men, the man Christ Jesus, who gave Himself as a ransom for all, the testimony given at the proper time. For this I was appointed a preacher and an apostle (I am telling the truth, I am not lying) as a teacher of the Gentiles in faith and truth" (1Ti. 2:1-7).

The Pillar and Support of the Truth

"I am writing these things to you, hoping to come to you before long; but in case I am delayed, I write so that you will know how one ought to conduct himself in the household of God, which is the church of the living God, the pillar and support of the truth. By common confession, great is the mystery of godliness: He who was revealed in the flesh, Was vindicated in the Spirit, Seen by angels, Proclaimed among the nations, Believed on in the world, Taken up in glory" (1Ti. 3:14-16).

Those Who Believe and Know the Truth

"But the Spirit explicitly says that in later times some will fall away from the faith, paying attention to deceitful spirits and doctrines of demons, by means of the hypocrisy of liars seared in their own conscience as with a branding iron, men who forbid marriage and advocate abstaining from foods which God has created to be gratefully shared in by those who believe and know the truth. For everything created by God is good, and nothing is to be rejected if it is received with gratitude; for it is sanctified by means of the word of God and prayer" (1Ti. 4:1-5).

Men of Depraved Mind and Deprived of the Truth

"If anyone advocates a different doctrine and does not agree with sound words, those of our Lord Jesus Christ, and with the doctrine conforming to godliness, he is conceited and understands nothing; but he has a morbid interest in controversial questions and disputes about words, out of which arise envy, strife, abusive language, evil suspicions, and constant friction between men of depraved mind and deprived of the truth, who suppose that godliness is a means of gain. But godliness actually is a means of great gain when accompanied by contentment. For we have brought nothing into the world, so we cannot take anything out of it either. If we have food and covering, with these we shall be content. But those who want to get rich fall into temptation and a snare and many foolish and harmful desires which plunge men into ruin and destruction. For the love of money is a root of all sorts of evil, and some by longing for it have wandered away from the faith and pierced themselves with many griefs" (1Ti. 6:3-10).

IN THE BOOK OF 2 TIMOTHY

Accurately Handling the Word of Truth

"Remind them of these things, and solemnly charge them in the presence of God not to wrangle about words, which is useless and leads to the ruin of the hearers. Be diligent to present yourself approved to God as a workman who does not need to be ashamed, accurately handling the word of truth. But avoid worldly and empty chatter, for it will lead to further ungodliness, and their talk will spread like gangrene. Among them are Hymenaeus and Philetus, men who have gone astray from the truth saying that the resurrection has already taken place, and they upset the faith of some. Nevertheless, the firm foundation of God stands, having this seal, 'The Lord knows those who are His,' and, 'Everyone who names the name of the Lord is to abstain from wickedness'" (2Ti. 2:14-19).

Chapter Two

Repentance Leading to the Knowledge of the Truth

"Now in a large house there are not only gold and silver vessels, but also vessels of wood and of earthenware, and some to honor and some to dishonor. Therefore, if anyone cleanses himself from these things, he will be a vessel for honor, sanctified, useful to the Master, prepared for every good work. Now flee from youthful lusts and pursue righteousness, faith, love and peace, with those who call on the Lord from a pure heart. But refuse foolish and ignorant speculations, knowing that they produce quarrels. The Lord's bond-servant must not be quarrelsome, but be kind to all, able to teach, patient when wronged, with gentleness correcting those who are in opposition, if perhaps God may grant them repentance leading to the knowledge of the truth, and they may come to their senses and escape from the snare of the devil, having been held captive by him to do his will" (2Ti. 2:20-26).

Never Able to Come to the Knowledge of the Truth

"But realize this, that in the last days difficult times will come. For men will be lovers of self, lovers of money, boastful, arrogant, revilers, disobedient to parents, ungrateful, unholy, unloving, irreconcilable, malicious gossips, without self-control, brutal, haters of good, treacherous, reckless, conceited, lovers of pleasure rather than lovers of God, holding to a form of godliness, although they have denied its power; Avoid such men as these. For among them are those who enter into households and captivate weak women weighed down with sins, led on by various impulses, always learning and never able to come to the knowledge of the truth. Just as Jannes and Jambres opposed Moses, so these men also oppose the truth, men of depraved mind, rejected in regard to the faith. But they will not make further progress; for their folly will be obvious to all, just as Jannes's and Jambres's folly was also. Now you followed my teaching, conduct, purpose, faith, patience, love, perseverance" (2Ti. 3:1-10).

Turn Away from the Truth and will Turn Aside to Myths

"I solemnly charge you in the presence of God and of Christ Jesus, who is to judge the living and the dead, and by His appearing and His kingdom: preach the word; be ready in season and out of season; reprove, rebuke, exhort, with great patience and instruction. For the time will come when they will not endure sound doctrine; but wanting to have their ears tickled, they will accumulate for themselves teachers in accordance to their own desires, and will turn away their ears from the truth and will turn aside to myths. But you, be sober in all things, endure hardship, do the work of an evangelist, fulfill your ministry" (2Ti. 4:1-5).

IN THE BOOK OF TITUS

Chosen of God and the Knowledge of the Truth

"Paul, a bond-servant of God and an apostle of Jesus Christ, for the faith of those chosen of God and the knowledge of the truth which is according to godliness, in the hope of eternal life, which God, who cannot lie, promised long ages ago, but at the proper time manifested, even His word, in the proclamation with which I was entrusted according to the commandment of God our Savior" (Tit. 1:1-3).

Men Who Turn Away from the Truth

"Who must be silenced because they are upsetting whole families, teaching things they should not teach for the sake of sordid gain. One of themselves, a prophet of their own, said, 'Cretans are always liars, evil beasts, lazy gluttons. This testimony is true. For this reason reprove them severely so that they may be sound in the faith, not paying attention to Jewish myths and commandments of men who turn away from the truth'" (Tit. 1:11-14).

IN THE BOOK OF HEBREWS

Sinning Willfully After Receiving the Truth

"For if we go on sinning willfully after receiving the knowledge of the truth, there no longer remains a sacrifice for sins, but a terrifying expectation of judgment and THE FURY OF A FIRE WHICH WILL CONSUME THE ADVERSARIES. Anyone who has set aside the Law of Moses dies without mercy on the testimony of two or three witnesses. How much severer punishment do you think he will deserve who has trampled under foot the Son of God, and has regarded as unclean the blood of the covenant by which he was sanctified, and has insulted the Spirit of grace? For we know Him who said, 'VENGEANCE IS MINE, I WILL REPAY.' And again, 'THE LORD WILL JUDGE HIS PEOPLE.' It is a terrifying thing to fall into the hands of the living God" (Heb. 10:26-31).

IN THE BOOK OF JAMES

He Brought Us Forth by the Word of Truth

"Blessed is a man who perseveres under trial; for once he has been approved, he will receive the crown of life which the Lord has promised to those who love Him. Let no one say when he is tempted, 'I am being tempted by God'; for God cannot be tempted by evil, and He

Himself does not tempt anyone. But each one is tempted when he is carried away and enticed by his own lust. Then when lust has conceived, it gives birth to sin; and when sin is accomplished, it brings forth death. Do not be deceived, my beloved brethren. Every good thing given and every perfect gift is from above, coming down from the Father of lights, with whom there is no variation or shifting shadow. In the exercise of His will He brought us forth by the word of truth, so that we would be a kind of first fruits among His creatures" (Jas. 1:12-18).

Do Not Be Arrogant and So Lie Against the Truth

"Who among you is wise and understanding? Let him show by his good behavior his deeds in the gentleness of wisdom. But if you have bitter jealousy and selfish ambition in your heart, do not be arrogant and so lie against the truth. This wisdom is not that which comes down from above, but is earthly, natural, demonic. For where jealousy and selfish ambition exist, there is disorder and every evil thing. But the wisdom from above is first pure, then peaceable, gentle, reasonable, full of mercy and good fruits, unwavering, without hypocrisy. And the seed whose fruit is righteousness is sown in peace by those who make peace" (Jas. 3:13-18).

Strays from the Truth and One Turns Him Back

"My brethren, if any among you strays from the truth and one turns him back, let him know that he who turns a sinner from the error of his way will save his soul from death and will cover a multitude of sins" (Jas. 5:19-20).

IN THE BOOK OF 1 PETER

In Obedience to the Truth Purified Your Souls

"Since you have in obedience to the truth purified your souls for a sincere love of the brethren, fervently love one another from the heart, for you have been born again not of seed which is perishable but imperishable, that is, through the living and enduring word of God. For, 'ALL FLESH IS LIKE GRASS, AND ALL ITS GLORY LIKE THE FLOWER OF GRASS. THE GRASS WITHERS, AND THE FLOWER FALLS OFF, BUT THE WORD OF THE LORD ENDURES FOREVER.' And this is the word which was preached to you" (1Pe. 1:22-25).

IN THE BOOK OF 2 PETER

Established in the Truth

"Therefore, I will always be ready to remind you of these things, even though you already know them, and have been established in the truth which is present with you. I consider it right, as long as I am in this earthly dwelling, to stir you up by way of reminder, knowing that the laying aside of my earthly dwelling is imminent, as also our Lord Jesus Christ has made clear to me. And I will also be diligent that at any time after my departure you will be able to call these things to mind" (2Pe. 1:12-15).

The Way of the Truth Will Be Maligned

"But false prophets also arose among the people, just as there will also be false teachers among you, who will secretly introduce destructive heresies, even denying the Master who bought them, bringing swift destruction upon themselves. Many will follow their sensuality, and because of them the way of the truth will be maligned;   and in their greed they will exploit you with false words; their judgment from long ago is not idle, and their destruction is not asleep" (2Pe. 2:1-3).

IN THE BOOK OF 1 JOHN

We Lie and Do Not Practice the Truth

"This is the message we have heard from Him and announce to you, that God is Light, and in Him there is no darkness at all. If we say that we have fellowship with Him and yet walk in the darkness, we lie and do not practice the truth; but if we walk in the Light as He Himself is in the Light, we have fellowship with one another, and the blood of Jesus His Son cleanses us from all sin. If we say that we have no sin, we are deceiving ourselves and the truth is not in us. If we confess our sins, He is faithful and righteous to forgive us our sins and to cleanse us from all unrighteousness. If we say that we have not sinned, we make Him a liar and His word is not in us" (1Jn. 1:5-10).

Is a Liar, and the Truth Is Not in Him

"By this we know that we have come to know Him, if we keep His commandments. The one who says, 'I have come to know Him,' and does not keep His commandments, is a liar, and the truth is not in him; but whoever keeps His word, in him the love of God has truly been perfected. By this we know that we are in Him: the one who says he abides in Him ought himself to walk in the same manner as He walked" (1Jn. 2:3-6).

Because You Do Not know the Truth

"Children, it is the last hour; and just as you heard that antichrist is coming, even now many antichrists have appeared; from this we know that it is the last hour. They went out from us, but they were not really of us; for if they had been of us, they would have remained with us; but they went out, so that it would be shown that they all are not of us. But you have an anointing from the Holy One, and you all know. I have not written to you because you do not know the truth, but because you do know it, and because no lie is of the truth. Who is the liar but the one who denies that Jesus is the Christ? This is the antichrist, the one who denies the Father and the Son. Whoever denies the Son does not have the Father; the one who confesses the Son has the Father also. As for you, let that abide in you which you heard from the beginning. If what you heard from the beginning abides in you, you also will abide in the Son and in the Father. This is the promise which He Himself made to us: eternal life" (1Jn. 2:18-25).

In Deed and Truth

"Do not be surprised, brethren, if the world hates you. We know that we have passed out of death into life, because we love the brethren. He who does not love abides in death. Everyone who hates his brother is a murderer; and you know that no murderer has eternal life abiding in him. We know love by this, that He laid down His life for us; and we ought to lay down our lives for the brethren. But whoever has the world's goods, and sees his brother in need and closes his heart against him, how does the love of God abide in him? Little children, let us not love with word or with tongue, but in deed and truth. We will know by this that we are of the truth, and will assure our heart before Him in whatever our heart condemns us; for God is greater than our heart and knows all things. Beloved, if our heart does not condemn us, we have confidence before God; and whatever we ask we receive from Him, because we keep His commandments and do the things that are pleasing in His sight" (1Jn. 3:13-22).

We Know the Spirit of Truth and the Spirit of Error

"Beloved, do not believe every spirit, but test the spirits to see whether they are from God, because many false prophets have gone out into the world. By this you know the Spirit of God: every spirit that confesses that Jesus Christ has come in the flesh is from God; and every spirit that does not confess Jesus is not from God; this is the spirit of the antichrist, of which you have heard that it is coming, and now it is already in the world. You are from God, little children, and have overcome them; because greater is He who is in you than he who is in the world. They are from the world; therefore they speak as from the world, and the world listens to them. We are from God; he who knows God listens to us; he who is not from God does not listen to us. By this we know the spirit of truth and the spirit of error" (1Jn. 4:1-6).

The Spirit Is the Truth

"Who is the one who overcomes the world, but he who believes that Jesus is the Son of God? This is the One who came by water and blood, Jesus Christ; not with the water only, but with the water and with the blood. It is the Spirit who testifies, because the Spirit is the truth. For there are three that testify: the Spirit and the water and the blood; and the three are in agreement. If we receive the testimony of men, the testimony of God is greater; for the testimony of God is this, that He has testified concerning His Son. The one who believes in the Son of God has the testimony in himself; the one who does not believe God has made Him a liar, because he has not believed in the testimony that God has given concerning His Son. And the testimony is this, that God has given us eternal life, and this life is in His Son. He who has the Son has the life; he who does not have the Son of God does not have the life" (1Jn. 5:5-12).

IN THE BOOK OF 2 JOHN

Not Only I, but Also All Who Know the Truth

"The elder to the chosen lady and her children, whom I love in truth; and not only I, but also all who know the truth, for the sake of the truth which abides in us and will be with us forever: Grace, mercy and peace will be with us, from God the Father and from Jesus Christ, the

Son of the Father, in truth and love" (2Jn. 1:1-3).

Walking in Truth

"I was very glad to find some of your children walking in truth, just as we have received commandment to do from the Father. Now I ask you, lady, not as though I were writing to you a new commandment, but the one which we have had from the beginning, that we love one another. And this is love, that we walk according to His commandments. This is the commandment, just as you have heard from the beginning, that you should walk in it" (2Jn. 1:4-6).

IN THE BOOK OF 3 JOHN

My Children Walking in the Truth

"The elder to the beloved Gaius, whom I love in truth. Beloved, I pray that in all respects you may prosper and be in good health, just as your soul prospers. For I was very glad when brethren came and testified to your truth, that is, how you are walking in truth. I have no greater joy than this, to hear of my children walking in the truth" (3Jn. 1:1-4).

Fellow Workers with the Truth

"Beloved, you are acting faithfully in whatever you accomplish for the brethren, and especially when they are strangers; and they have testified to your love before the church. You will do well to send them on their way in a manner worthy of God. For they went out for the sake of the Name, accepting nothing from the Gentiles. Therefore we ought to support such men, so that we may be fellow workers with the truth" (3Jn. 1:5-8).

From the Truth Itself

"Beloved, do not imitate what is evil, but what is good. The one who does good is of God; the one who does evil has not seen God. Demetrius has received a good testimony from everyone, and from the truth itself; and we add our testimony, and you know that our testimony is true" (3Jn. 1:11-12).

WISDOM IN THE NEW TESTAMENT

WISDOM IN THE BOOK OF MATTHEW

Wisdom Is vindicated by Her Deeds

"But to what shall I compare this generation? It is like children sitting in the market places, who call out to the other children, and say, 'We played the flute for you, and you did not dance; we sang a dirge, and you did not mourn.' For John came neither eating nor drinking, and they say, 'He has a demon!' The Son of Man came eating and drinking, and they say, 'Behold, a gluttonous man and a drunkard, a friend of tax collectors and sinners!' Yet wisdom is vindicated by her deeds" (Mt. 11:16-19).

The Ends of the Earth to Hear the Wisdom

"Then some of the scribes and Pharisees said to Him, 'Teacher, we want to see a sign from You.' But He answered and said to them, 'An evil and adulterous generation craves for a sign; and yet no sign will be given to it but the sign of Jonah the prophet; for just as JONAH WAS THREE DAYS AND THREE NIGHTS IN THE BELLY OF THE SEA MONSTER, so will the Son of Man be three days and three nights in the heart of the earth. The men of Nineveh will stand up with this generation at the judgment, and will condemn it because they repented at the preaching of Jonah;

and behold, something greater than Jonah is here. The Queen of the South will rise up with this generation at the judgment and will condemn it, because she came from the ends of the earth to hear the wisdom of Solomon; and behold, something greater than Solomon is here'" (Mt. 12:38-42).

Where Did This Man Get This Wisdom

"When Jesus had finished these parables, He departed from there. He came to His hometown and began teaching them in their synagogue, so that they were astonished, and said, 'Where did this man get this wisdom and these miraculous powers? Is not this the carpenter's son? Is not His mother called Mary, and His brothers, James and Joseph and Simon and Judas? And His sisters, are they not all with us? Where then did this man get all these things?' And they took offense at Him. But Jesus said to them, 'A prophet is not without honor except in his hometown and in his own household.' And He did not do many miracles there because of their unbelief" (Mt. 13:53-58).

WISDOM IN THE BOOK OF MARK

What Is This Wisdom Given to Him

"Jesus went out from there and came into His hometown; and His disciples followed Him.

When the Sabbath came, He began to teach in the synagogue; and the many listeners were astonished, saying, "Where did this man get these things, and what is this wisdom given to Him, and such miracles as these performed by His hands? Is not this the carpenter, the son of Mary, and brother of James and Joses and Judas and Simon? Are not His sisters here with us?" And they took offense at Him. Jesus said to them, "A prophet is not without honor except in his hometown and among his own relatives and in his own household." And He could do no miracle there except that He laid His hands on a few sick people and healed them. And He wondered at their unbelief. And He was going around the villages teaching. (Mk. 6:1-6).

WISDOM IN THE BOOK OF LUKE

To Grow and Become Strong, Increasing in Wisdom

"When they had performed everything according to the Law of the Lord, they returned to Galilee, to their own city of Nazareth. The Child continued to grow and become strong, increasing in wisdom; and the grace of God was upon Him" (Lk. 2:39-40).

Chapter Three

Kept Increasing in Wisdom and Stature

"And Jesus kept increasing in wisdom and stature, and in favor with God and men" (Lk. 2:52).

Yet Wisdom Is Vindicated by All Her Children

"To what then shall I compare the men of this generation, and what are they like? They are like children who sit in the market place and call to one another, and they say, 'We played the flute for you, and you did not dance; we sang a dirge, and you did not weep.' For John the Baptist has come eating no bread and drinking no wine, and you say, 'He has a demon!' The Son of Man has come eating and drinking, and you say, 'Behold, a gluttonous man and a drunkard, a friend of tax collectors and sinners!' Yet wisdom is vindicated by all her children" (Lk. 7:31-35).

The Wisdom of God

"One of the lawyers said to Him in reply, 'Teacher, when You say this, You insult us too.' But He said, 'Woe to you lawyers as well! For you weigh men down with burdens hard to bear, while you yourselves will not even touch the burdens with one of your fingers. Woe to you! For you build the tombs of the prophets, and it was your fathers who killed them. So you are witnesses and approve the deeds of your fathers;

because it was they who killed them, and you build their tombs. For this reason also the wisdom of God said, 'I will send to them prophets and apostles, and some of them they will kill and some they will persecute, so that the blood of all the prophets, shed since the foundation of the world, may be charged against this generation, from the blood of Abel to the blood of Zechariah, who was killed between the altar and the house of God; yes, I tell you, it shall be charged against this generation." Woe to you lawyers! For you have taken away the key of knowledge; you yourselves did not enter, and you hindered those who were entering'" (Lk. 11:45-52).

I Will Give You Utterance and Wisdom

"But before all these things, they will lay their hands on you and will persecute you, delivering you to the synagogues and prisons, bringing you before kings and governors for My name's sake. It will lead to an opportunity for your testimony. So make up your minds not to prepare beforehand to defend yourselves; for I will give you utterance and wisdom which none of your opponents will be able to resist or refute. But you will be betrayed even by parents and brothers and relatives and friends, and they will put some of you to death, and you will be hated by all because of My name. Yet not a hair of your head will perish. By your endurance you will gain your lives" (Lk. 21:12-19).

Chapter Three

WISDOM IN THE BOOK OF ACTS

Full of the Spirit and of Wisdom

"Now at this time while the disciples were increasing in number, a complaint arose on the part of the Hellenistic Jews against the native Hebrews, because their widows were being overlooked in the daily serving of food. So the twelve summoned the congregation of the disciples and said, 'It is not desirable for us to neglect the word of God in order to serve tables. Therefore, brethren, select from among you seven men of good reputation, full of the Spirit and of wisdom, whom we may put in charge of this task. But we will devote ourselves to prayer and to the ministry of the word.' The statement found approval with the whole congregation; and they chose Stephen, a man full of faith and of the Holy Spirit, and Philip, Prochorus, Nicanor, Timon, Parmenas and Nicolas, a proselyte from Antioch. And these they brought before the apostles; and after praying, they laid their hands on them" (Ac. 6:1-6).

They Were Unable to Cope with the Wisdom

"And Stephen, full of grace and power, was performing great wonders and signs among the people. But some men from what was called the Synagogue of the Freedmen, including both Cyrenians and Alexandrians, and some from

Cilicia and Asia, rose up and argued with Stephen. But they were unable to cope with the wisdom and the Spirit with which he was speaking. Then they secretly induced men to say, 'We have heard him speak blasphemous words against Moses and against God.' And they stirred up the people, the elders and the scribes, and they came up to him and dragged him away and brought him before the Council. They put forward false witnesses who said, 'This man incessantly speaks against this holy place and the Law; for we have heard him say that this Nazarene, Jesus, will destroy this place and alter the customs which Moses handed down to us'" (Ac. 6:8-14).

Granted Him Favor and Wisdom

"The patriarchs became jealous of Joseph and sold him into Egypt. Yet God was with him, and rescued him from all his afflictions, and granted him favor and wisdom in the sight of Pharaoh, king of Egypt, and he made him governor over Egypt and all his household" (Ac. 7:9-10).

WISDOM IN THE BOOK OF ROMANS

The Riches Both of Wisdom and Knowledge

"Oh, the depth of the riches both of the wisdom and knowledge of God! How unsearchable are His judgments and unfathomable His ways! For WHO HAS KNOWN THE MIND OF THE LORD, OR WHO BECAME HIS COUNSELOR? Or WHO HAS FIRST GIVEN TO HIM THAT IT MIGHT BE PAID BACK TO HIM AGAIN? For from Him and through Him and to Him are all things. To Him be the glory forever. Amen!" (Ro. 11:33-36).

WISDOM IN THE BOOK OF 1 CORINTHIANS

Not With Wisdom of Words

"Now I plead with you, brethren, by the name of our Lord Jesus Christ, that you all speak the same thing, and that there be no divisions among you, but that you be perfectly joined together in the same mind and in the same judgment. For it has been declared to me concerning you, my brethren, by those of Chloe's household, that there are contentions among you. Now I say this, that each of you says, 'I am of Paul,' or 'I am of Apollos,' or 'I am of Cephas,' or 'I am of Christ.' Is Christ divided? Was Paul crucified for you? Or were you baptized in the name of Paul? I thank God that I baptized none of you except Crispus and Gaius, lest anyone should say that I had baptized in my own name. Yes, I also baptized the household of Stephanas. Besides, I do not know whether I baptized any other. For Christ did not send me to baptize, but to preach the gospel, not with wisdom of words, lest the cross of Christ should be made of no effect" (1

Cor. 1:10-17).

Who Became for Us Wisdom

"For the message of the cross is foolishness to those who are perishing, but to us who are being saved it is the power of God. For it is written: 'I will destroy the wisdom of the wise, And bring to nothing the understanding of the prudent.' Where is the wise? Where is the scribe? Where is the disputer of this age? Has not God made foolish the wisdom of this world? For since, in the wisdom of God, the world through wisdom did not know God, it pleased God through the foolishness of the message preached to save those who believe. For Jews request a sign, and Greeks seek after wisdom; but we preach Christ crucified, to the Jews a stumbling block and to the Greeks foolishness, but to those who are called, both Jews and Greeks, Christ the power of God and the wisdom of God. Because the foolishness of God is wiser than men, and the weakness of God is stronger than men. For you see your calling, brethren, that not many wise according to the flesh, not many mighty, not many noble, are called. But God has chosen the foolish things of the world to put to shame the wise, and God has chosen the weak things of the world to put to shame the things which are mighty; and the base things of the world and the things which are despised God has chosen, and the things which are not, to bring to nothing the things that are, that no flesh should glory in His presence. But of Him you are in Christ Jesus, who became for us wisdom from God — and righteousness and sanctification and redemption — that, as it is written, 'He who glories, let him glory in the Lord'" (1 Co. 1:18-31).

Not with Persuasive Words of Human Wisdom

"And I, brethren, when I came to you, did not come with excellence of speech or of wisdom declaring to you the testimony of God. For I determined not to know anything among you except Jesus Christ and Him crucified. I was with you in weakness, in fear, and in much trembling. And my speech and my preaching were not with persuasive words of human wisdom, but in demonstration of the Spirit and of power, that your faith should not be in the wisdom of men but in the power of God" (1 Co. 2:1-5).

We Speak the Wisdom of God in a Mystery

"However, we speak wisdom among those who are mature, yet not the wisdom of this age, nor of the rulers of this age, who are coming to nothing. But we speak the wisdom of God in a mystery, the hidden wisdom which God ordained before the ages for our glory, which none of the rulers of this age knew; for had they known, they would not have crucified the Lord of glory. But as it is written: 'Eye has not seen, nor ear heard, nor have entered into the heart of man The things which God has prepared for those who love Him.' But God has revealed them to us through His Spirit. For the Spirit searches all things, yes, the deep things of God. For what man knows the things of a man except the spirit of the man which is in him? Even so no one knows the things of God except the Spirit of God. Now we have received, not the spirit of the world, but the Spirit who is from God, that we might know the things that have been freely given to us by God. These things we also speak, not in words which man's wisdom teaches but which the Holy Spirit teaches, comparing spiritual things with spiritual" (1 Co. 2:6-13).

To Be Wise in This Age

"Let no one deceive himself. If anyone among you seems to be wise in this age, let him become a fool that he may become wise. For the wisdom of this world is foolishness with God. For it is written, 'He catches the wise in their own craftiness'; and again, 'The Lord knows the thoughts of the wise, that they are futile.' Therefore let no one boast in men. For all things are yours: whether Paul or Apollos or Cephas, or the world or life or death, or things present or things to come—all are yours. And you are Christ's, and Christ is God's" (1 Co. 3:18-23).

Chapter Three

The Word of Wisdom through the Spirit

"There are diversities of gifts, but the same Spirit. There are differences of ministries, but the same Lord. And there are diversities of activities, but it is the same God who works all in all. But the manifestation of the Spirit is given to each one for the profit of all: for to one is given the word of wisdom through the Spirit, to another the word of knowledge through the same Spirit, to another faith by the same Spirit, to another gifts of healings by the same Spirit, to another the working of miracles, to another prophecy, to another discerning of spirits, to another different kinds of tongues, to another the interpretation of tongues. But one and the same Spirit works all these things, distributing to each one individually as He wills" (1 Co. 12:4-11).

WISDOM IN THE BOOK OF 2 CORINTHIANS

Not with Fleshly Wisdom but by the Grace of God

"For our boasting is this: the testimony of our conscience that we conducted ourselves in the world in simplicity and godly sincerity, not with fleshly wisdom but by the grace of God, and more abundantly toward you. For we are not writing any other things to you than what you read or understand. Now I trust you will understand, even to the end (as also you have understood us in part), that we are your boast as you also are ours, in the day of the Lord Jesus" (2 Co. 1:12-14).

WISDOM IN THE BOOK OF EPHESIANS

To Abound Toward Us in All Wisdom and Prudence

"Blessed be the God and Father of our Lord Jesus Christ, who has blessed us with every spiritual blessing in the heavenly places in Christ, just as He chose us in Him before the foundation of the world, that we should be holy and without blame before Him in love, having predestined us to adoption as sons by Jesus Christ to Himself, according to the good pleasure of His will, to the praise of the glory of His grace, by which He has made us accepted in the Beloved. In Him we have redemption through His blood, the forgiveness of sins, according to the riches of His grace which He made to abound toward us in all wisdom and prudence, having made known to us the mystery of His will, according to His good pleasure which He purposed in Himself, that in the dispensation of the fullness of the times He might gather together in one all things in Christ, both which are in heaven and which are on earth—in Him. In Him also we have obtained an inheritance, being predestined according to the purpose of Him who works all things according to the counsel of His will that we who first trusted in Christ should be to the praise of His glory. In Him you also trusted, after you heard the word of truth, the gospel of your salvation; in whom also, having believed, you were sealed with the Holy Spirit of promise, who is the guarantee of our inheritance until the redemption of the purchased possession, to the praise of His glory" (Eph. 1:3-14).

Give to You the Spirit of Wisdom and Revelation

"Therefore I also, after I heard of your faith in the Lord Jesus and your love for all the saints, do not cease to give thanks for you, making mention of you in my prayers: that the God of our Lord Jesus Christ, the Father of glory, may give to you the spirit of wisdom and revelation in the knowledge of Him, the eyes of your understanding being enlightened; that you may know what is the hope of His calling, what are the riches of the glory of His inheritance in the saints, and what is the exceeding greatness of His power toward us who believe, according to the working of His mighty power which He worked in Christ when He raised Him from the dead and seated Him at His right hand in the heavenly places, far above all principality and power and might and dominion, and every name that is named, not only in this age but also in that which is to come. And He put all things under His feet, and gave Him to be head over all things to the church, which is His body, the fullness of Him who fills all in all" (Eph. 1:15-23).

The Manifold Wisdom of God

"For this reason I, Paul, the prisoner of Christ Jesus for you Gentiles — if indeed you have heard of the dispensation of the grace of God which was given to me for you, how that by revelation He made known to me the mystery (as I have briefly written already, by which, when you read, you may understand my knowledge in the mystery of Christ), which in other ages was not made known to the sons of men, as it has now been revealed by the Spirit to His holy apostles and prophets: that the Gentiles should be fellow heirs, of the same body, and partakers of His promise in Christ through the gospel, of which I became a minister according to the gift of the grace of God given to me by the effective working of His power. To me, who am less than the least of all the saints, this grace was given, that I should preach among the Gentiles the unsearchable riches of Christ, and to make all see what is the fellowship of the mystery, which from the beginning of the ages has been hidden in God who created all things through Jesus Christ; to the intent that now the manifold wisdom of God might be made known by the church to the principalities and powers in the heavenly places, according to the eternal purpose which He accomplished in Christ Jesus our Lord, in whom we have boldness and access with confidence through faith in Him. Therefore I ask that you do not lose heart at my tribulations for you, which is your glory" (Eph. 3:1-13).

WISDOM IN THE BOOK OF COLOSSIANS

In All Wisdom and Spiritual Understanding

"For this reason we also, since the day we heard it, do not cease to pray for you, and to ask that you may be filled with the knowledge of His will in all wisdom and spiritual understanding; that you may walk worthy of the Lord, fully pleasing Him, being fruitful in every good work and increasing in the knowledge of God; strengthened with all might, according to His glorious power, for all patience and longsuffering with joy; giving thanks to the Father who has qualified us to be partakers of the inheritance of the saints in the light. He has delivered us from the power of darkness and conveyed us into the kingdom of the Son of His love, in whom we have redemption through His blood, the forgiveness of sins" (Col. 1:9-14).

Teaching Every Man in All Wisdom

"I now rejoice in my sufferings for you, and fill up in my flesh what is lacking in the afflictions of Christ, for the sake of His body, which is the church, of which I became a minister according to the stewardship from God which was given to me for you, to fulfill the word of God, the mystery which has been hidden from ages and from generations, but now has been revealed to His saints. To them God willed to make known what are the riches of the glory of this mystery among the Gentiles: which is Christ in you, the hope of glory. Him we preach, warning every man and teaching every man in all wisdom, that we may present every man perfect in Christ Jesus. To this end I also labor, striving according to His working which works in me mightily" (Col. 1:24-29).

In Whom Are Hidden All the Treasures of Wisdom

"For I want you to know what a great conflict I have for you and those in Laodicea, and for as many as have not seen my face in the flesh, that their hearts may be encouraged, being knit together in love, and attaining to all riches of the full assurance of understanding, to the knowledge of the mystery of God, both of the Father and of Christ, in whom are hidden all the treasures of wisdom and knowledge. Now this I say lest anyone should deceive you with persuasive words. For though I am absent in the flesh, yet I am with you in spirit, rejoicing to see your good order and the steadfastness of your faith in Christ" (Col. 2:1-5).

Chapter Three

An Appearance of Wisdom in Self-imposed Religion

"Therefore, if you died with Christ from the basic principles of the world, why, as though living in the world, do you subject yourselves to regulations—'Do not touch, do not taste, do not handle,' which all concern things which perish with the using—according to the commandments and doctrines of men? These things indeed have an appearance of wisdom in self-imposed religion, false humility, and neglect of the body, but are of no value against the indulgence of the flesh" (Col. 2:20-23).

Dwell in You Richly in all Wisdom

"Therefore, as the elect of God, holy and beloved, put on tender mercies, kindness, humility, meekness, longsuffering; bearing with one another, and forgiving one another, if anyone has a complaint against another; even as Christ forgave you, so you also must do. But above all these things put on love, which is the bond of perfection. And let the peace of God rule in your hearts, to which also you were called in one body; and be thankful. Let the word of Christ dwell in you richly in all wisdom, teaching and admonishing one another in psalms and hymns and spiritual songs, singing with grace in your hearts to the Lord. And whatever you do in word or deed, do all in the name of the Lord Jesus,

giving thanks to God the Father through Him"
(Col. 3:12-17).

Walk in Wisdom

"Walk in wisdom toward those who are
outside, redeeming the time. Let your speech
always be with grace, seasoned with salt, that you
may know how you ought to answer each one"
(Col. 4:5-6).

WISDOM IN THE BOOK OF JAMES

If Any of You Lacks Wisdom, Let Him
Ask of God

"If any of you lacks wisdom, let him ask of
God, who gives to all liberally and without
reproach, and it will be given to him. But let him
ask in faith, with no doubting, for he who doubts
is like a wave of the sea driven and tossed by the
wind. For let not that man suppose that he will
receive anything from the Lord; he is a double-
minded man, unstable in all his ways" (Jas. 1:5-8).

In the Meekness of Wisdom

"Who is wise and understanding among
you? Let him show by good conduct that his
works are done in the meekness of wisdom. But if
you have bitter envy and self-seeking in your
hearts, do not boast and lie against the truth. This

wisdom does not descend from above, but is earthly, sensual, demonic. For where envy and self-seeking exist, confusion and every evil thing are there. But the wisdom that is from above is first pure, then peaceable, gentle, willing to yield, full of mercy and good fruits, without partiality and without hypocrisy. Now the fruit of righteousness is sown in peace by those who make peace" (Jas. 3:13-18).

WISDOM IN THE BOOK OF 2 PETER

According to the Wisdom Given to Him

"Therefore, beloved, looking forward to these things, be diligent to be found by Him in peace, without spot and blameless; and consider that the longsuffering of our Lord is salvation — as also our beloved brother Paul, according to the wisdom given to him, has written to you, as also in all his epistles, speaking in them of these things, in which are some things hard to understand, which untaught and unstable people twist to their own destruction, as they do also the rest of the Scriptures. You therefore, beloved, since you know this beforehand, beware lest you also fall from your own steadfastness, being led away with the error of the wicked; but grow in the grace and knowledge of our Lord and Savior Jesus Christ. To Him be the glory both now and forever. Amen" (2 Pe. 3:14-18).

WISDOM IN THE BOOK OF REVELATION

To Receive Power and Riches and Wisdom

"Then I looked, and I heard the voice of many angels around the throne, the living creatures, and the elders; and the number of them was ten thousand times ten thousand, and thousands of thousands, saying with a loud voice: 'Worthy is the Lamb who was slain To receive power and riches and wisdom, And strength and honor and glory and blessing!' And every creature which is in heaven and on the earth and under the earth and such as are in the sea, and all that are in them, I heard saying: 'Blessing and honor and glory and power Be to Him who sits on the throne, And to the Lamb, forever and ever!' Then the four living creatures said, 'Amen!' And the twenty-four elders fell down and worshiped Him who lives forever and ever" (Rev. 5:11-14).

Blessing and Glory and Wisdom and Honor

"After these things I looked, and behold, a great multitude which no one could number, of all nations, tribes, peoples, and tongues, standing before the throne and before the Lamb, clothed with white robes, with palm branches in their hands, and crying out with a loud voice, saying, 'Salvation belongs to our God who sits on the throne, and to the Lamb!' All the angels stood around the throne and the elders and the four living creatures, and fell on their faces before the throne and worshiped God, saying: 'Amen! Blessing and glory and wisdom, thanksgiving and honor and power and might, be to our God forever and ever. Amen'" (Rev. 7:9-12).

Here Is Wisdom

"Then I saw another beast coming up out of the earth, and he had two horns like a lamb and spoke like a dragon. And he exercises all the authority of the first beast in his presence, and causes the earth and those who dwell in it to worship the first beast, whose deadly wound was healed. He performs great signs, so that he even makes fire come down from heaven on the earth in the sight of men. And he deceives those who dwell on the earth by those signs which he was granted to do in the sight of the beast, telling those who dwell on the earth to make an image to the beast who was wounded by the sword and lived. He was granted power to give breath to the image of the beast, that the image of the beast should both speak and cause as many as would not worship the image of the beast to be killed. He causes all, both small and great, rich and poor, free and slave, to receive a mark on their right hand or on their foreheads, and that no one may buy or sell except one who has the mark or the name of the beast, or the number of his name. Here is wisdom. Let him who has understanding calculate the number of the beast, for it is the number of a man: His number is 666" (Rev. 13:11-18).

Here Is the Mind Which Has Wisdom

"The beast that you saw was, and is not, and will ascend out of the bottomless pit and go to perdition. And those who dwell on the earth will marvel, whose names are not written in the Book of Life from the foundation of the world, when they see the beast that was, and is not, and yet is. Here is the mind which has wisdom: The seven heads are seven mountains on which the woman sits. There are also seven kings. Five have fallen, one is, and the other has not yet come. And when he comes, he must continue a short time. And the beast that was, and is not, is himself also the eighth, and is of the seven, and is going to perdition. The ten horns which you saw are ten kings who have received no kingdom as yet, but they receive authority for one hour as kings with the beast. These are of one mind, and they will give their power and authority to the beast. These will make war with the Lamb, and the Lamb will overcome them, for He is Lord of lords and King of kings; and those who are with Him are called, chosen, and faithful" (Rev. 17:8-14).

Chapter Four

INSTRUCTION IN THE NEW TESTAMENT

Whatever Was Written in Earlier Times Was Written For our Instruction

"Now we who are strong ought to bear the weaknesses of those without strength and not just please ourselves. Each of us is to please his neighbor for his good, to his edification. For even Christ did not please Himself; but as it is written, 'THE REPROACHES OF THOSE WHO REPROACHED YOU FELL ON ME.' For whatever was written in earlier times was written for our instruction, so that through perseverance and the encouragement of the Scriptures we might have hope. Now may the God who gives perseverance and encouragement grant you to be of the same mind with one another according to Christ Jesus, so that with one accord you may with one voice glorify the God and Father of our Lord Jesus Christ" (Ro. 15:1-6).

For Our Instruction

"Now these things happened as examples for us, so that we would not crave evil things as they also craved. Do not be idolaters, as some of them were; as it is written, 'THE PEOPLE SAT DOWN TO EAT AND DRINK, AND STOOD UP TO PLAY.' Nor let us act immorally, as some of them did, and twenty-three thousand fell in one day. Nor let us try the Lord, as some of them did, and were destroyed by the serpents. Nor grumble, as some of them did, and were destroyed by the destroyer. Now these things happened to them as an example, and they were written for our instruction, upon whom the ends of the ages have come. Therefore let him who thinks he stands take heed that he does not fall. No temptation has overtaken you but such as is common to man; and God is faithful, who will not allow you to be tempted beyond what you are able, but with the temptation will provide the way of escape also, so that you will be able to endure it" (1Co. 10:6-13).

But In Giving This Instruction, I Do Not Praise You

"But in giving this instruction, I do not praise you, because you come together not for the better but for the worse. For, in the first place, when you come together as a church, I hear that divisions exist among you; and in part I believe it. For there must also be factions among you, so that those who are approved may become evident among you. Therefore when you meet together, it is not to eat the Lord's Supper, for in your eating each one takes his own supper first; and one is hungry and another is drunk. What! Do you not have houses in which to eat and drink? Or do you despise the church of God and shame those who have nothing? What shall I say to you? Shall I praise you? In this I will not praise you" (1Co.

11:17-22).

Bring Them Up In the Discipline and Instruction of the Lord

"Fathers, do not provoke your children to anger, but bring them up in the discipline and instruction of the Lord" (Eph. 6:4).

You Received From Us Instruction as To How You Ought to Walk

"Finally then, brethren, we request and exhort you in the Lord Jesus, that as you received from us instruction as to how you ought to walk and please God (just as you actually do walk), that you excel still more. For you know what commandments we gave you by the authority of the Lord Jesus. For this is the will of God, your sanctification; that is, that you abstain from sexual immorality; that each of you know how to possess his own vessel in sanctification and honor, not in lustful passion, like the Gentiles who do not know God; and that no man transgress and defraud his brother in the matter because the Lord is the avenger in all these things, just as we also told you before and solemnly warned you. For God has not called us for the purpose of impurity, but in sanctification. So, he who rejects this is not rejecting man but the God who gives His Holy Spirit to you" (1Th. 4:1-8).

Have Charge Over You in the Lord and Give You Instruction

"But we request of you, brethren, that you appreciate those who diligently labor among you, and have charge over you in the Lord and give you instruction, and that you esteem them very highly in love because of their work. Live in peace with one another. We urge you, brethren, admonish the unruly, encourage the fainthearted, help the weak, be patient with everyone. See that no one repays another with evil for evil, but always seek after that which is good for one another and for all people. Rejoice always; pray without ceasing; in everything give thanks; for this is God's will for you in Christ Jesus. Do not quench the Spirit; do not despise prophetic utterances. But examine everything carefully; hold fast to that which is good; abstain from every form of evil" (1Th. 5:12-22).

If They Do Not Obey Our Instruction Do Not Associate With Him

"If anyone does not obey our instruction in this letter, take special note of that person and do not associate with him, so that he will be put to shame. Yet do not regard him as an enemy, but admonish him as a brother" (2Th. 3:14-15).

The Goal of Our Instruction Is Love

"As I urged you upon my departure for Macedonia, remain on at Ephesus so that you may instruct certain men not to teach strange doctrines, nor to pay attention to myths and endless genealogies, which give rise to mere speculation rather than furthering the administration of God which is by faith. But the goal of our instruction is love from a pure heart and a good conscience and a sincere faith. For some men, straying from these things, have turned aside to fruitless discussion, wanting to be teachers of the Law, even though they do not understand either what they are saying or the matters about which they make confident assertions" (1Ti. 1:3-7).

Quietly Receive Instruction with Entire Submissiveness

"Therefore I want the men in every place to pray, lifting up holy hands, without wrath and dissension. Likewise, I want women to adorn themselves with proper clothing, modestly and discreetly, not with braided hair and gold or pearls or costly garments, but rather by means of good works, as is proper for women making a claim to godliness. A woman must quietly receive instruction with entire submissiveness. But I do not allow a woman to teach or exercise authority over a man, but to remain quiet. For it was Adam who was first created, and then Eve. And it was not Adam who was deceived, but the woman being deceived, fell into transgression. But women will be preserved through the bearing of children if they continue in faith and love and sanctity with self-restraint" (1Ti. 2:8-15).

With Great Patience and Instruction

"I solemnly charge you in the presence of God and of Christ Jesus, who is to judge the living and the dead, and by His appearing and His kingdom: preach the word; be ready in season and out of season; reprove, rebuke, exhort, with great patience and instruction. For the time will come when they will not endure sound doctrine; but wanting to have their ears tickled, they will accumulate for themselves teachers in accordance to their own desires, and will turn away their ears from the truth and will turn aside to myths. But you, be sober in all things, endure hardship, do the work of an evangelist, fulfill your ministry" (2Ti. 4:1-5).

Instruction About Washings and Laying On Of Hands

"Therefore leaving the elementary teaching about the Christ, let us press on to maturity, not laying again a foundation of repentance from dead works and of faith toward God, of instruction about washings and laying on of hands, and the resurrection of the dead and eternal judgment.

And this we will do, if God permits. For in the case of those who have once been enlightened and have tasted of the heavenly gift and have been made partakers of the Holy Spirit, and have tasted the good word of God and the powers of the age to come, and then have fallen away, it is impossible to renew them again to repentance, since they again crucify to themselves the Son of God and put Him to open shame. For ground that drinks the rain which often falls on it and brings forth vegetation useful to those for whose sake it is also tilled, receives a blessing from God; but if it yields thorns and thistles, it is worthless and close to being cursed, and it ends up being burned" (Heb. 6:1-8).

UNDERSTANDING IN THE NEW TESTAMENT

Jesus Said, "Are You Still Lacking in Understanding Also"?

"Peter said to Him, 'Explain the parable to us.' Jesus said, 'Are you still lacking in understanding also? Do you not understand that everything that goes into the mouth passes into the stomach, and is eliminated? But the things that proceed out of the mouth come from the heart, and those defile the man. For out of the heart come evil thoughts, murders, adulteries, fornications, thefts, false witness, slanders. These are the things which defile the man; but to eat with unwashed hands does not defile the man'" (Mt. 15:15-20).

You Are Mistaken, Not Understanding the Scriptures

"But Jesus answered and said to them, 'You are mistaken, not understanding the Scriptures nor the power of God. For in the resurrection they neither marry nor are given in marriage, but are like angels in heaven. But regarding the resurrection of the dead, have you not read what was spoken to you by God: 'I AM THE GOD OF ABRAHAM, AND THE GOD OF ISAAC, AND THE GOD OF JACOB'? He is not the God of the dead but of the living. When the crowds heard this, they were astonished at His teaching" (Mt. 22:29-33).

With All the Understanding

"One of the scribes came and heard them arguing, and recognizing that He had answered them well, asked Him, 'What commandment is the foremost of all?' Jesus answered, 'The foremost is, 'HEAR, O ISRAEL! THE LORD OUR GOD IS ONE LORD; AND YOU SHALL LOVE THE LORD YOUR GOD WITH ALL YOUR HEART, AND WITH ALL YOUR SOUL, AND WITH ALL YOUR MIND, AND WITH ALL YOUR STRENGTH.' The second is this, 'YOU SHALL LOVE YOUR NEIGHBOR AS YOURSELF.' There is no other commandment greater than these.' The scribe said to Him, 'Right, Teacher; You have truly stated that HE IS ONE, AND THERE IS NO ONE ELSE BESIDES HIM; AND TO LOVE HIM WITH ALL THE HEART AND WITH ALL THE UNDERSTANDING AND WITH ALL THE STRENGTH, AND TO LOVE ONE'S NEIGHBOR AS HIMSELF, is much more than all burnt offerings and sacrifices.' When Jesus saw that he had answered intelligently, He said to him, 'You are not far from the kingdom of God.' After that, no one would venture to ask Him any more questions" (Mr. 12:28-34).

Chapter Five

All Who Heard Him Were Amazed at His Understanding

"Now His parents went to Jerusalem every year at the Feast of the Passover. And when He became twelve, they went up there according to the custom of the Feast; and as they were returning, after spending the full number of days, the boy Jesus stayed behind in Jerusalem. But His parents were unaware of it, but supposed Him to be in the caravan, and went a day's journey; and they began looking for Him among their relatives and acquaintances. When they did not find Him, they returned to Jerusalem looking for Him. Then, after three days they found Him in the temple, sitting in the midst of the teachers, both listening to them and asking them questions. And all who heard Him were amazed at His understanding and His answers. When they saw Him, they were astonished; and His mother said to Him, 'Son, why have You treated us this way? Behold, Your father and I have been anxiously looking for You.' And He said to them, 'Why is it that you were looking for Me? Did you not know that I had to be in My Father's house?' But they did not understand the statement which He had made to them. And He went down with them and came to Nazareth, and He continued in subjection to them; and His mother treasured all these things in her heart" (Lu. 2:41-51).

Chapter Five

Without Understanding

"And just as they did not see fit to acknowledge God any longer, God gave them over to a depraved mind, to do those things which are not proper, being filled with all unrighteousness, wickedness, greed, evil; full of envy, murder, strife, deceit, malice; they are gossips, slanderers, haters of God, insolent, arrogant, boastful, inventors of evil, disobedient to parents, without understanding, untrustworthy, unloving, unmerciful; and although they know the ordinance of God, that those who practice such things are worthy of death, they not only do the same, but also give hearty approval to those who practice them" (Ro. 1:28-32).

By a Nation Without Understanding Will I Anger You

"But I say, surely they have never heard, have they? Indeed they have; 'THEIR VOICE HAS GONE OUT INTO ALL THE EARTH, AND THEIR WORDS TO THE ENDS OF THE WORLD.' But I say, surely Israel did not know, did they? First Moses says, 'I WILL MAKE YOU JEALOUS BY THAT WHICH IS NOT A NATION, BY A NATION WITHOUT UNDERSTANDING WILL I ANGER YOU.' And Isaiah is very bold and says, 'I WAS FOUND BY THOSE WHO DID NOT SEEK ME, I BECAME MANIFEST TO THOSE WHO DID NOT ASK FOR ME.' But as for

Israel He says, 'ALL THE DAY LONG I HAVE STRETCHED OUT MY HANDS TO A DISOBEDIENT AND OBSTINATE PEOPLE'" (Ro. 10:18-21).

Being Darkened In Their Understanding, Excluded From the Life of God

"So this I say, and affirm together with the Lord, that you walk no longer just as the Gentiles also walk, in the futility of their mind, being darkened in their understanding, excluded from the life of God because of the ignorance that is in them, because of the hardness of their heart; and they, having become callous, have given themselves over to sensuality for the practice of every kind of impurity with greediness. But you did not learn Christ in this way, if indeed you have heard Him and have been taught in Him, just as truth is in Jesus, that, in reference to your former manner of life, you lay aside the old self, which is being corrupted in accordance with the lusts of deceit, and that you be renewed in the spirit of your mind, and put on the new self, which in the likeness of God has been created in righteousness and holiness of the truth" (Eph. 4:17-24).

The Knowledge of His Will In All Spiritual Wisdom and Understanding

"For this reason also, since the day we heard of it, we have not ceased to pray for you and to ask that you may be filled with the knowledge of His will in all spiritual wisdom and understanding, so that you will walk in a manner worthy of the Lord, to please Him in all respects, bearing fruit in every good work and increasing in the knowledge of God; strengthened with all power, according to His glorious might, for the attaining of all steadfastness and patience; joyously giving thanks to the Father, who has qualified us to share in the inheritance of the saints in Light. For He rescued us from the domain of darkness, and transferred us to the kingdom of His beloved Son, in whom we have redemption, the forgiveness of sins" (Col. 1:9-14).

The Wealth That Comes From the Full Assurance of Understanding

"For I want you to know how great a struggle I have on your behalf and for those who are at Laodicea, and for all those who have not personally seen my face, that their hearts may be encouraged, having been knit together in love, and attaining to all the wealth that comes from the full assurance of understanding, resulting in a true knowledge of God's mystery, that is, Christ Himself, in whom are hidden all the treasures of wisdom and knowledge. I say this so that no one will delude you with persuasive argument. For even though I am absent in body, nevertheless I am with you in spirit, rejoicing to see your good discipline and the stability of your faith in Christ" (Col. 2:1-5).

The Lord Will Give You Understanding in Everything

"You therefore, my son, be strong in the grace that is in Christ Jesus. The things which you have heard from me in the presence of many witnesses, entrust these to faithful men who will be able to teach others also. Suffer hardship with me, as a good soldier of Christ Jesus. No soldier in active service entangles himself in the affairs of everyday life, so that he may please the one who enlisted him as a soldier. Also if anyone competes as an athlete, he does not win the prize unless he competes according to the rules. The hard-working farmer ought to be the first to receive his share of the crops. Consider what I say, for the Lord will give you understanding in everything" (2Ti. 2:1-7).

Who Among You Is Wise and Understanding?

"Who among you is wise and understanding? Let him show by his good behavior his deeds in the gentleness of wisdom. But if you have bitter jealousy and selfish ambition in your heart, do not be arrogant and so lie against the truth. This wisdom is not that which comes down from above, but is earthly, natural, demonic. For where jealousy and selfish ambition exist, there is disorder and every evil thing. But the wisdom from above is first pure, then peaceable, gentle, reasonable, full of mercy and good fruits, unwavering, without hypocrisy. And the seed whose fruit is righteousness is sown in peace by those who make peace" (Jas. 3:13-18).

Live With Your Wives in an Understanding Way

"You husbands in the same way, live with your wives in an understanding way, as with someone weaker, since she is a woman; and show her honor as a fellow heir of the grace of life, so that your prayers will not be hindered" (1Pe. 3:7).

He Has Given Us Understanding So That We May Know Him

"We know that no one who is born of God sins; but He who was born of God keeps him, and the evil one does not touch him. We know that we are of God, and that the whole world lies in the power of the evil one. And we know that the Son of God has come, and has given us understanding so that we may know Him who is true; and we are in Him who is true, in His Son Jesus Christ. This is the true God and eternal life" (1Jn. 5:18-20).

Chapter Five

Let Him Who Has Understanding Calculate the Number of the Beast

"Then I saw another beast coming up out of the earth; and he had two horns like a lamb and he spoke as a dragon. He exercises all the authority of the first beast in his presence. And he makes the earth and those who dwell in it to worship the first beast, whose fatal wound was healed. He performs great signs, so that he even makes fire come down out of heaven to the earth in the presence of men. And he deceives those who dwell on the earth because of the signs which it was given him to perform in the presence of the beast, telling those who dwell on the earth to make an image to the beast who *had the wound of the sword and has come to life. And it was given to him to give breath to the image of the beast, so that the image of the beast would even speak and cause as many as do not worship the image of the beast to be killed. And he causes all, the small and the great, and the rich and the poor, and the free men and the slaves, to be given a mark on their right hand or on their forehead, and he provides that no one will be able to buy or to sell, except the one who has the mark, either the name of the beast or the number of his name. Here is wisdom. Let him who has understanding calculate the number of the beast, for the number is that of a man; and his number is six hundred and sixty-six" (Rev. 13:11-18).

DAILY FAITH CONFESSIONS

(These are not direct quotations from the Bible but are paraphrased confessions based on scripture.)
SAY THEM OUT LOUD.

I am God's child (Jn. 1:12). I am royalty (1 Pet. 2:9). I am hidden with Christ in God (Col. 3:3). I am united with the Lord (1 Cor. 6:17). I am a friend of Christ (Jn. 15:15). I am raised up with Him, and seated with Him in heavenly places in Christ Jesus (Eph. 2:6). I was bought with a price (1 Cor. 6:19-20). I am blessed when I come in, and blessed shall I be when I go out (Deut. 28:6). I am a personal witness of Christ (Acts 1:8). I am a saint who prays in the Holy Spirit to keep myself in the love of God (Jude 1:20-21). I draw near with confidence to the throne of grace (Heb. 4:16). I have been adopted by the Father (Eph. 1:5). I am the salt and light of the earth (Mt. 5:13). I am the head and not the tail, and I am above, and not underneath. I am the lender and not the borrower (Deut. 28:13). I have authority to trample serpents and scorpions and over all the power of the enemy (Lk. 10:19). I am a member of the body of Christ (1 Cor. 12:27). God blessed me to be fruitful, and multiply, and replenish the earth, and subdue it: and have dominion (Gen. 1:28). I cannot be separated from God's love (Ro. 8:39). The good work God has begun in me will be perfected (Phil. 1:5). I can do all things through Christ who strengthens me (Phil. 4:13). No weapon that is formed against me will prosper (Is. 54:17). So then faith cometh by hearing, and hearing by the word of God (Ro. 10:17 KJV). Faith is my currency to operate in the kingdom of God (Ro. 14:23). I am God's workmanship created in Christ Jesus for good works, which God prepared beforehand (Eph. 2:10). I have been appointed to bear fruit, and that my fruit would remain (Jn. 15:16). I am being wise when I am winning souls for King Jesus (Pr. 11:30). My body is the temple of the Holy Spirit (1 Cor. 6:19). I have access to God through the Holy Spirit (Eph. 2:18). I have been justified (Ro. 5:1). Therefore there is now no condemnation for those who are in Christ Jesus (Ro. 8:1). Greater is He who is in me than he who is in the world (1 Jn. 4:4). I will do greater works than Jesus because He went to the Father (Jn. 14:12). As God was with Moses, He will be with me; God will not fail me or forsake me (Jos. 1:5). I see myself the way God see me. God sees me as a king (Gen, 17:6, Rev. 1:6) God sees me as royalty (1 Pet. 2:9). God sees me as the righteousness of God in Christ, bold as a lion (Ro. 3:22, Pr. 28:1). God sees me without spot or wrinkle because of the blood of Jesus (1 Pet. 1:19). I am having faith for big things because God owns everything and I'm His son (Ps. 24:1). No man will be able to stand before me all the days of my life (Jos. 1:5). My Father is glorified by this that I bear much fruit, and proves I'm a disciple (see Jn. 15:8). I think big and confess big things because God is big (Ps. 24:1). I will respect God for the big God that He is and my mouth will create whatever I want (Lk. 6:45). I no longer think of millions, my renewed mind thinks of billions because the wealth of the wicked is laid up for the righteous (Pr. 13:22). The sinner's job is to gather and collect for the one who is good in God's sight (Ecc. 2:26). Redemption is not complete without prosperity. Jesus hung on the cross so I can have the whole package, not just salvation (2 Cor. 8:9). I don't have to qualify, Jesus has qualified me. Jesus reversed the curse. The devil is a liar, and Jesus is the Messiah. Jesus is made unto to me wisdom, righteousness, sanctification, and redemption (1 Cor. 1:30). I submit to God, I resist the devil and he flees from me (Jas. 4:7). For God has not given me the spirit of fear; but of power, and of love, and of a sound mind (2 Tim. 1:7). The Holy Spirit will teach me all things (Jn. 14:26). The Holy Spirit will guide me into all truth (Jn.16:13). The Holy Spirit abides in me, and I don't need anyone to teach me, but the anointing teaches me all things (1 Jn. 2:27). I quench fiery darts from the wicked one with the shield of faith (Eph. 6:16). I stand firm against the schemes of the devil (Eph. 6:11). I already have the victory and Satan cannot back me up. I hold my position of consistent victory after victory (2 Cor. 2:14). I walk in love and live by faith (Gal. 5:6). I have been redeemed from the curse of the law, poverty, sickness, and spiritual death (Gal. 3:13; Deut. 28). I will bear so much fruit. I'm God's workmanship created beforehand for good works (Eph. 2:10). God's favor is on my life (Ps. 3:8). God blesses me and His favor surrounds me as with a shield (Ps. 5:12). The kingdom of God is within me (Lk. 17:21). I have a production plant inside of me that bears fruit to change the world (Gen. 1:28). God gives me power to get wealth to establish His covenant on earth (Deut. 8:18). I am blessed to be a blessing (Gen. 12:2). I have Satan on the run. I will make a mockery of him (Jas. 4:7). Thank you, Father; your angels keep me in all my ways (Ps. 91:11). The world and the kingdom of darkness are no match for me!

PRAY FOR SALVATION

Say the following prayer out loud.

Heavenly Father, I am a sinner and I need a Savior. I confess Jesus Christ as the Lord of my life. I repent of all my sins. Father, I truly believe you raised Jesus from the dead. Father, give me spiritual hunger to spend time in Your Word day and night so my mind is renewed. I understand that by meditating and submitting to Your Word daily I will be transformed into the image of Jesus, day-by-day. Thank you, Father, for Your goodness, mercy, and grace. I pray in Jesus' name. Amen.

PRAYER FOR BAPTISM OF THE HOLY SPIRIT

Say the following prayer out loud.

Father, I am your child because Jesus is my Lord. Jesus said, "How much more shall your heavenly Father give the Holy Spirit to those who ask Him." I ask you now in the name of Jesus to fill me with the Holy Spirit. Thank you, Father, I received the baptism of the Holy Spirit by faith. I yield my vocal organs and expect to speak in tongues as the Holy Spirit gives me utterance in Jesus name. Father, I plan to pray in the Holy Spirit building myself up on my most holy faith, and keep myself in the love of God, as mentioned in Jude 20 and 21. In Jesus name I decree it. Amen.

ABOUT THE AUTHOR

Eugene Carvalho is the founder of Receiving by Faith. He is an administrator and Christian author of seventy-seven books. God uses him in the offices of pastor, evangelist and prophet. He holds a bachelor's degree in biblical studies and a double minor in pastoral ministry and world missions. He also holds a master's degree in practical theology. Eugene prayed for a translator and God sent his wife Mercedes who has a six- year degree in Spanish from a university in Tampico, Mexico. They have participated in evangelism in the streets of Mexico for many years. They have also traveled to churches all over the United States and Mexico winning souls and preaching the gospel of the kingdom. Visit their ministry website at: www.receivingbyfaith.org.

BOOKS BY EUGENE IN ENGLISH

For a complete list of books by Eugene Carvalho visit receivingbyfaith.org or amazon.com.

Receiving by Faith
Faith for Every Day: 365 Daily Devotions
Faith Cometh by Hearing, and Hearing by the
Word of God
Faith, Hope, and Love
Walk in Love and Live by Faith
Topical Christian Handbook and Scripture Guide
The Gospel Is the Power of God unto Salvation
Seed Time and Harvest Time
Your New Identity in Christ
The Cross and the Blood
The Holy Spirit
The Attributes of God
The Favor of God
The Glory of God
The Grace of God
The Love of God
The Power of God
The Promises of God
The Spirit of God
The Throne of God
The New Testament Church: A Survey from the
Book of Ephesians
Vengeance and Recompense
God's Angel's
Prayer and Fasting
God's Mighty Prophets

BOOKS BY EUGENE IN SPANISH

Las Promesas de Dios
Los Salmos de David
Lo Sobrenatural: Lo que la Bíblia Tiene que Decir
Una Mirada Topica Del Libro De Los Salmos
Dios es Amor: Lo que la Biblia Tiene que Decir
La Adquisición de la Sabiduría es Vital: Lo que la
Biblia Tiene que Decir

NOTES

NOTES

<u>NOTES</u>

152